Founder/Editor-in-Chief: Kate E. Hinshaw
Editors: Andi Avery, Hogan Seidel, Gabby Follett
Cover design: Amina Gingold
Interior design: Kate E.Hinshaw
Analog Cookbook Logo: Sarah Lawrence's Design Emporium
Questions: hello@analogcookbook.com

Letter from the editors

Dear readers,

This week marks 20 years since hurricane Katrina. The original copies of Helen Hill's Recipes for Disaster, the legendary text which this publication grows from, was destroyed in the storm along with many of Hill's films. A post hurricane Recipes for Disaster was made and Hill began the publication with a letter dated November 16th, 2005. She starts:

"Since moving to New Orleans five years ago, my husband Paul and I had become part of a fun, progressive, and artistic community. I never expected that it could all disappear so quickly. When Hurricane Katrina hit, our friends were scattered everywhere. It has been a strange, surreal time. But people are already coming together in surprising ways to help out and rebuild. This new edition of Recipes for Disaster is a case in point."

I often think about the quote by psychoanalyst D.W. Winnicott–"it is a joy to be hidden and a disaster not to be found." There is so much freedom in making analog and experimental films in part because you can do it alone in a studio, bathroom, kitchen, and use household materials. Often it is about play and process more than results. At the same time, filmmaking and making art can feel incredibly lonely at times. Starting with a new medium can feel overwhelming. Asking for help, and opening yourself up to collaboration can feel deeply vulnerable. Still, there can be joy in finding others who do the same thing we do–collaborations spark, you share ideas and film stock, and suddenly you're no longer making work in solitude.

The letter Hill wrote from her parent's house as a self-described "New Orleans exile" reaches out to others in her community in a time of devastation, tragedy, confusion, loneliness and neglect of those affected by Katrina. Thirty-seven artists came together to share their recipes for filmmaking in Recipes for Disaster–an act of kindness for others looking to learn from their artistic processes. Hill ends her letter:

"When I first made this book, the whole point was to bring together the scattered community of artists making handmade films. These folks are creative pioneers, inventing their own recipes and methods. Hundreds more have written me for their own copy of Recipes for Disaster, and so this community quietly grows."

It's been a two year hiatus since our last issue of Analog Cookbook and a lot has changed since 2023. The idea for All Recipes came out of a need to reset–to remember why we do this, and embrace community. I am deeply moved by every artist in this issue who has shared their process for art making. Each recipe shared is an act of kindness.

Today, as the world moves on to new disasters, the shadow of Katrina still looms large for some. I often wonder what Hill would think of Analog Cookbook if she were alive today. Every issue we think of her incredible work. The world feels deeply unkind in this current moment. Still, our community quietly grows with love and care for one another.

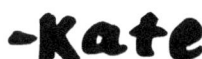

ALTERNATIVE CHEMICAL RECIPES

Expired-ol (16)

Will De Ritter is a London-based filmmaker. He works with celluloid film and photochemicals to produce films which tread a fine line between experimental and genre movies. He is interested in working with obsolete photographic technology to produce effects which are digitally unachievable, and developing sustainable solutions to photographic practices.

Will De Ritter

Developer C (20)

Alexandra (Alex) Monaghan is a young student filmmaker interested in every facet of filmmaking. Focusing primarily on directing and cinematography, Alex is largely interested in representation on screen, but also analysing the depths of which the cinema camera influences the spectator in creating narrative meaning of a piece. Alex fell in love with film as a teenager when she would buy broken 35mm still cameras from thrift shops, and would try and repair them - to varying degrees of success. Fascinated still by the form of analogue filmmaking, Alex has made unimaginable strides in filmmaking since then; from presenting her academic work in Smith College; to showcasing her documentary "STRIKE!" in film festivals all over Ireland and Toronto; to creating a 16mm expanded film installation sculpture at Hampshire College about experiential memory, this may be Alexandra's first foray into 16mm film, but it certainly will not be her last.

Alexandra (Alex) Monaghan

Eco-Reversal for B&W 16mm Film (Ginkgo Leaf Developer) (26)

Hogan Seidel is a Boston-based artist working in the traditions of experimental film and photography. Their current artistic research, framed through poetic, political, and personal lenses, delves into contemporary queer discourse, queer history, and queer ecology. Hogan currently is an assistant teaching professor of photography at Simmons University.

Hogan Seidel

So Salty (32)

Fabian Heller is an artist working in all sorts of media both analog and digital. In his work he is constantly looking for new methods of image creation, whether it be trough pixel-shifting algorithms on screen or experimental exposure methods on film. Currently, Heller is compiling an encyclopedia of all possible images, develops an algae-based method for sustainable image reproduction, and plans to fight the sun with a knife. He graduated in Fine Arts at the artschool of Kassel as a so called 'Meisterschüler' and is currently enrolled in the post graduation program at the Academy for Media Arts Cologne.

Fabian Heller

B/W alt-developers from our Bombay neighborhood (36)

Karan is a filmmaker and founder of photo-chemical lab and alt performance space Harkat Studios in Mumbai India. His work revolves around new ways of seeing, material memory – especially its cinematic forms, the possibilities of handmade photochemistry including 19th century silver based processes and finding mediums for stories.

Karan Suri Talwar, Simran Ankolkar and Namrata Sanghani of the Harkat Lab.

ANALOG SOUND RECIPES

Inflammatoire (hand-crafted 16mm sound) (44)

Nicole Blundell is a bilingual artist working on film and living in Ottawa. Her films have been shown nationally and internationally, Ann Arbour film festival (USA), WNDX (Winnipeg), TAIS Animation showcase (Toronto) Paris Film art Festival (France), Festival du film Canadien À Dieppe (Canada), Rendez vous Québec Cinéma (Montreal), Festival International du film francophone (Toronto) Engauge Experimental film festival (Seattle, USA) and the International Experimental Film Festival (Athens, Greece)

Nicole Blundell

DIY 16mm Optical Sound Recorder (48)

Hrvoje Spudić (b. 1987) graduated from the School of Architecture in Zagreb, Croatia, in 2015. He works as an assistant at the Cabinet for Drawing and Design, where his practice explores techniques and technologies of print, photography, film, and light phenomena. He is a member of Klubvizija film lab and serves as a technical advisor and expanded cinema assistant at the 25fps festival. His work spans sound-on-film experiments (Sound Analysis, Experiment in the Reproduction of Sound), rotating camera/projector systems (the Rotoprojector series), camera obscura installations (the Translations series, in collaboration with Sara Salamon), and light-based performance and installation pieces (1m² of Light, 1m² of Gold, with Sven Sorić). He is currently developing a DIY CNC-controlled optical printer/film scanner/subtitle engraver, using a modified 16mm Bolex and a hacked Siemens 2000 projector.

Hrvoje Spudic

Test 1 (Solar-powered sound) (54)

Test 1 is a direct animation 16mm film that is accompanied by live sound performance, where the sounds are coming from the devices that transfer light into the sound.

Asel Bakchakova

DIY Optical Soundtrack (58)

Dominick Rivers is an experimental moving-image artist, musician, and educator. His video work, framed by larger installations, examines the popular media used to capture and sentimentalize memory. His research is focused on developing eco-friendly substitutions for alternative photographic processes that can be implemented with motion-picture film. These substitutions demonstrate that commonly accepted techniques can be made more accessible, promote environmental sustainability, and remain emotionally exigent. His contributions to the analog film community have led to performances, workshops, exhibitions, and residencies for Mono No Aware XVI (Brooklyn), LIFT (Toronto), CICA New Media Arts Conference (Seoul), and No Name Cinema (Santa Fe).

Dominick Rivers

Home Print Making

Cyanotype on Film (62)

徐璐 Erica Sheu is a Los Angeles-based Taiwanese filmmaker who makes experimental short films exploring the synesthetic qualities of memory, guided by feelings and emotions. Sheu had taught personal filmmaking workshops at the Academy Museum, and DIY celluloid filmmaking workshops at Mono No Aware, T.A.P.E Los Angeles (hosting at Whammy! Analog Media).

Erica Sheu

Midsummer (16mm cyanotype) (70)

Masha Vlasova is an award-winning experimental and non-fiction filmmaker. She has exhibited and screened her films at Ann Arbor Film Festival, Chicago Underground Film Festival, Smack Mellon, Anthology Archives, Abrons Arts Center, the Border Project Gallery in New York City, Vox Populi in Philadelphia, and Carpenter Center for the Visual Arts at Harvard University, among others. She's a MacDowell Fellow and a Fulbright Fellow. Her recent film "Un-Tidal" received two awards for "Original Concept" and "Best Celluloid Film" at Experimental Film Festival of East Anglia, UK. She teaches film production at Oxford College of Emory University and lives in Atlanta, GA.

Masha Vlasova, Anna Guan

Testosterone Gel as Film Soup + Watergrams on Film (78)

Born and raised in western Washington, Avian de Keizer is an interdisciplinary visual artist whose work centers on techniques in experimental photographic processes. He has been studying media arts since 2017 and delved into everything from video news production to video essays on popular culture. Avian was on the President's List at South Puget Sound Community College for multiple quarters and received an Associate of Arts degree in 2023. While Avian studied film production for around 5 years, pivoting towards visual art has allowed him to be less afraid of expressing his identity and diving into themes related to that identity. His current artistic research dives into memory, repair, identity, anonymity, gender, and environment. He is particularly interested in abstract direct animation as a way to express various experiences of identity to an audience. He believes the participatory and sensory elements of experimental film lend themselves to shared experiences.

Avian de Keizer

Gang Sync Contact Printer (82)

Charlotte is a process. They are an experimental animator and documentary filmmaker whose research centers around community building through media making. They hold a BA from the University of Florida, and an MFA in Film and Video Production from the University of Iowa. They are the co-founder and President of Mechanical Eye Microcinema, a non-profit that aims to create equitable access to filmmaking, where they collaboratively organize Fierce Flix, a social justice project that provides mentorship, film education, and leadership development to trans, nonbinary, queer, and femme youth. Charlotte currently teaches Media Arts at Warren Wilson College.

Charlotte Taylor

Playing with Process

Pseudo Solarization on B&W Reversal film using C4 processing

(88)

MaLo Sutra Fish is a French visual artist currently based in Paris, born in 1985. Her practice is set between the USA - mostly the East Coast - and France, and focuses on her passion for film as a format and material through Photography and Filmmaking. She currently is a member at the cinema collective L'Etna (France), at the art collective Flux Factory (USA) and partial member of Gowanus Darkroom (USA) and regularly collaborates with AgX (USA). Her prior areas of focus are collaborations particularly in short film and music video making. Her current work with the moving image includes a trilogy in association with Isao Yamada; Super 8 music videos made in collaboration with US Independent Music Scene (Osees, Flat Worms, + more), known as the "Performance Series". Her latest photographic series focus on the different aesthetics of memory - "the images we have in our brains" - studying and experimenting processing and printing techniques.

MaLo Sutra Fish

Dried Flowers (Emulsion Lift)

(96)

Amelia Mevers is a multimedia artist from Atlanta, Georga. She produces work across mediums with a particular interest in oil pastel portraiture, collage, and film. Currently an undergraduate at Emory university's oxford collage she aims to merge an interdisciplinary education with artistic practice. Amelia's work focuses on themes of gender, personal identity and the power of imagined futures.

Amelia Mevers

253' 11" (live experimental film instructions) (98)

Auden Lincoln-Vogel is a filmmaker whose work spans both animation and live action. Although the majority of his films are narrative, every once in a while someone forgets to lock the door and he gets into the scritchy-scratchy 16mm tinker-toy potion stuff. When they find him, they immediately wash him off, change the locks, and make him read Syd Field until he recants. He currently lives in Iowa City where he and his partner in cinematic crime, Philip Rabalais, run Osline Pictures and get up to no good.

Auden Lincoln-Vogel

above/below or How to Create a Rotoscope Animation with a Bolex Mattebox (102)

Anna Hogg is an artist and filmmaker whose practice indulges in the impossible and the unknowable, exploring these fields as productive sites for play and wild flights of imagination. Allowing truth to be unstable and knowledge to be indeterminate, her work "stays with the trouble" of the impossible and the unknowable. She is interested in the ways technology–including that of cinema, the archive, or even surveillance technology–forms memory, knowledge, and regimes of truth. In particular, she investigates technology's gaps, dissonances, limits, and failures, beyond which one may speculate alternate ways of knowing and understanding, or even revel in the unknowability of such a space. Storytelling itself becomes the framework for analysis and critical engagement, often using the framework of Ursula K. LeGuin's carrier bag theory of fiction as a point of departure.

Anna Hogg

How to make animation into a sewing circle

(114)

Charlie Wilcox is a embroiderist-animator who hails from Lindstrom, Minnesota, also known as "America's Little Sweden." Charlie's social practice involves exploring what it means to turn the creation of animation into a hands-on event that can focalize and generate community. By developing animation into a collaborative act that integrates qualities from textile craftwork and participatory art, Charlie explores new situations and purposes for animation as a method for collective expression and visioning. His work creates methodologies for representations of social design and collaboration that favor embodied realities beyond sheer logicism and consensus. Charlie makes his own embroidered animations, curates and organizes the From Below Microcinema, helps organize Portland Textile Month, works in the performing arts departments at Reed College, and plays tuba in the punk band Horsebag.

Charlie Wilcox

- -

Cover Design

Amina Gingold is a photographer, filmmaker, and bookmaker based in New York, NY. Her work explores gut instincts, misremembering, and the complexities of uncovering the truth. She holds a BFA in Photography and Video from the School of Visual Arts and completed the one-year Matte Institute Free School of Photography (2023–2024). Amina's work has been shortlisted for the Palm Photo Prize (2022) and featured in Lenscratch. She has exhibited and screened at the Film-Makers' Cooperative, Millennium Film Workshop, Bulegoa Z/B, Documenta Madrid, Mono No Aware, SoMad, Flat Earth Cinema, and 10 14 Gallery. Her recent residencies include Brooklyn Darkroom's Traveling Artist Program (2024), WORTHLESSSTUDIOS' Mobile Darkroom Airstream Trailer (2024), and Gowanus Darkroom (2025).

Amina Gingold

Alternate CHEMICAL RECIPES

DIY recipes with ingredients found at home or at your local dispensary.

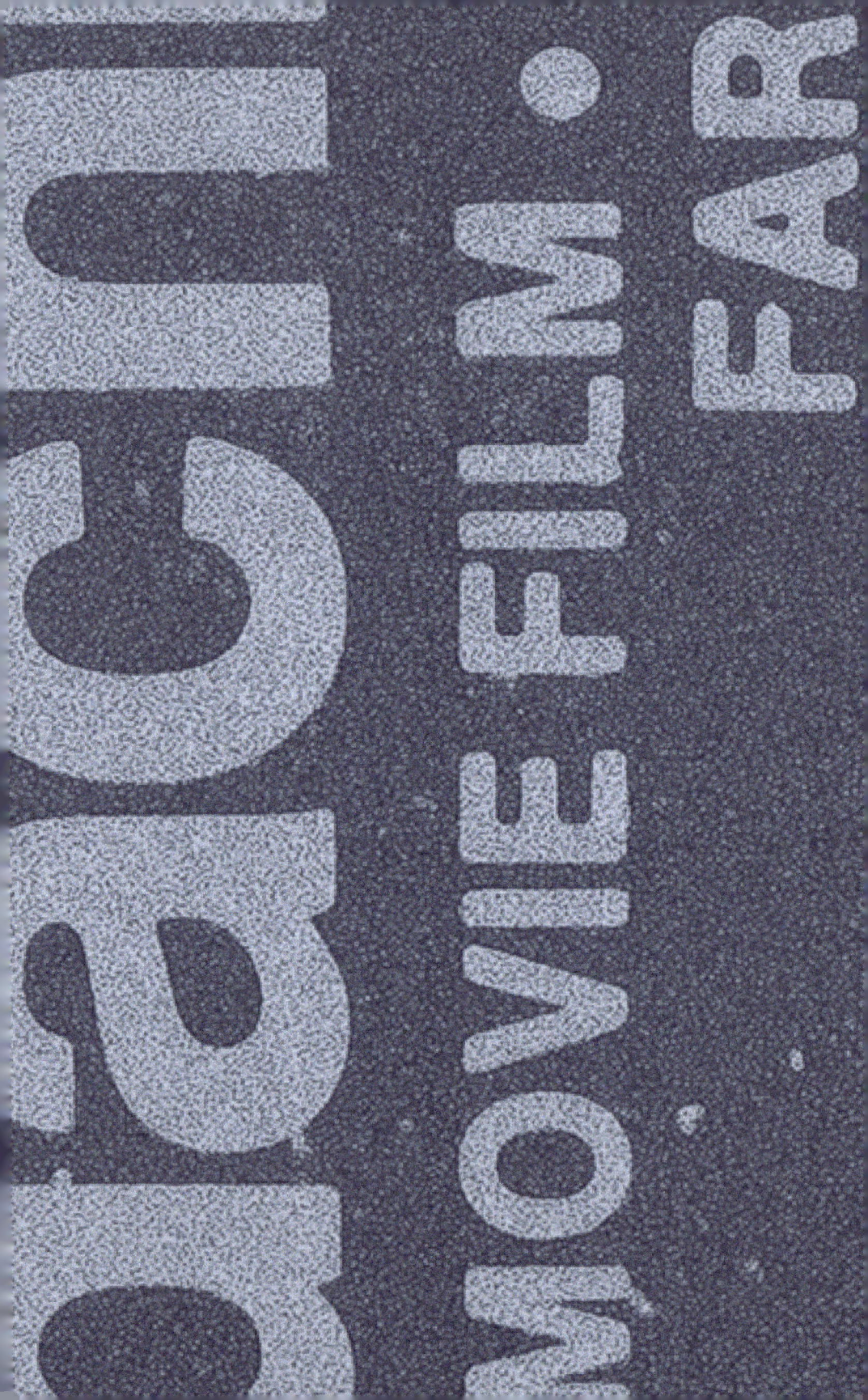

Expired-ol

The Japanese proverb mottainai (勿体無い) expresses the regret of something being discarded needlessly. It can be translated literally as "don't be wasteful."

My first rolls of Kodachrome came from an uneducated purchase; it was 2019 and I had little appreciation of the degradation that occurs as film ages, or the inability of modern film labs to process it. I just saw some cheap film that had presumably sat in the back of a drawer for decades, waiting to fulfil its potential.

Those rolls sat dormant on my shelf for nearly 4 years until I had built some confidence in hand processing Super 8 in caffenol using the spaghetti method (see Analog Cookbook Issue 2, page 57). On a very bright summer day I took a roll of 1978 expired Kodachrome 40 down to the beach and overexposed it by at least 5 stops (one for each decade past the expiration date). I wish I could say that first roll was a success, but my best attempts yielded a dense pitch black negative. It didn't go to waste; it works great as black leader.

By this time I knew it was possible to develop expired Kodachrome as a black and white negative. I had heard rodinal might work well, but one shot developers have never appealed to me. However, deterred by my initial failure, I placed my second exposed roll back on the shelf to rest for another year.

Delving into the back of my fridge one evening, I was hit by the pungent odor of rotting spinach. I always buy spinach with the best intentions, but after cooking one curry, I invariably neglect the unused leftovers until they are no longer fit for human consumption. As the expired leaf burnt hairs in my nostrils, I was reminded of a workshop I had seen given by Dagie Brundert for Baltic Analog Lab. The bitter smell indicated the presence of phenolic acids, electron-rich chemicals which could be used as a mild reducing agent, and thereby convert exposed silver halides into visible metallic silver. After conducting a little research, I discovered that spinach does indeed contain the phenolic compounds ortho-coumaric acid, ferulic acid, and para-coumaric acid, among others.

As the spinach was expired and decomposing, any phenolic content would have been breaking down and diminishing. Still, I was intrigued enough to test the viability of a spinach developer.

Will De Ritter

Here is my recipe for expired spinach-ol:

Stuff a jar full of expired leftover spinach.

Fill the jar with boiling water and leave to steep overnight.

In the morning, strain the spinach water and discard the leaves; all the useful phenols have been extracted.

For 1 liter of spinach water add:

→ 24g (12 teaspoons) of sodium carbonate
→ 20g (3 teaspoons) of vitamin C

Develop for 10 – 15 minutes at room temperature.

To my surprise and delight, the expired spinach-ol worked wonders on 1978-expired Kodachrome, producing a clear base and very fine grain—and to think I stumbled onto this solution all thanks to poor meal planning. The decreased phenolic content of the decomposing plants theoretically produces a weaker developer, resulting in less aggressive development of potentially fogged areas of film. Heavily overexposing the film compensated for this underdevelopment, as well as the loss in light sensitivity. In a very real sense, it is the quality of being expired which allows both film and developer to synergize, bringing new life to each other.

As more leafy vegetables and herbs expired in my fridge I began to test them as Kodachrome developers. Bas-ol (basil) and dill-ol also produced acceptable images from long-expired Kodachrome.

This isn't to say that you will always get fantastic results with Kodachrome in expired phenol-based developers. Results will vary greatly depending on how the film has been stored over the years, which is usually unknown—but adopting a mottainai mindset can lead to unexpectedly effective darkroom solutions while reducing food waste.

4 Tips for Processing Expired Kodachrome

1.Overexpose and underdevelop

As film ages, the silver halides are gradually exposed to thermal degradation and background radiation, which results in a loss of light sensitivity and denser base layer on the film, manifesting as "fogging" on the image. Overexposing (one stop for each decade past the film's expiration date, as a general rule) helps to compensate for that loss of light sensitivity, while underdeveloping or "pulling"* film results in a thinner base layer and reduced base fog.

Bonus tip: if dealing with very heavy base fog, consider adding iodized salt to the developer, which acts as a restrainer - 12g or 2 ½ teaspoons per liter should do it.

2. Develop as a negative

Kodachrome is a very simple film designed for a very complicated process (K-14, which is now defunct). It is not compatible with modern color processes (C41/ECN-2/E6), but can still be processed as B+W negative or reversal. Even though Kodachrome is a reversal film, I would advise developing as a negative over reversal. This is because reversal processing effectively reduces a film's exposure latitude in order to produce a high contrast print which can be projected. Reversal processing is therefore unforgiving on incorrect exposure. As we are estimating our film's speed, it would be helpful to retain as much of the film's exposure latitude as possible. A negative B+W process will result in a lower contrast negative, but will give the highest chance of producing an acceptable image.

3. Test your developing times

Unless we have acquired a batch of stock which we know has been stored together, every expired film we shoot will have had a different journey before landing in our cameras. Testing a short strip of film before committing to developing a whole roll could save some heartache. In complete darkness, find an inch-long strip from a section of film which should contain an exposure. Develop the strip at a normal developing time and observe the result. If unsure, try pushing/pulling further strips until a desired time is found.

4. Don't overpay

We can ask an eBay seller how a film has been stored, but we can never know for sure. I would avoid trying to find film at flea markets, as leaving film sitting in the sun for hours on end is not the best way to preserve its light sensitivity. As a general rule I don't like to pay more than around £5 or $7 for an old roll of Kodachrome. Film is expensive enough without inflating the secondary market.

*Pulling film means rating it at a lower ISO and developing it for less time to for many reasons including; getting softer contrast, smoother tones, and more detail in bright areas

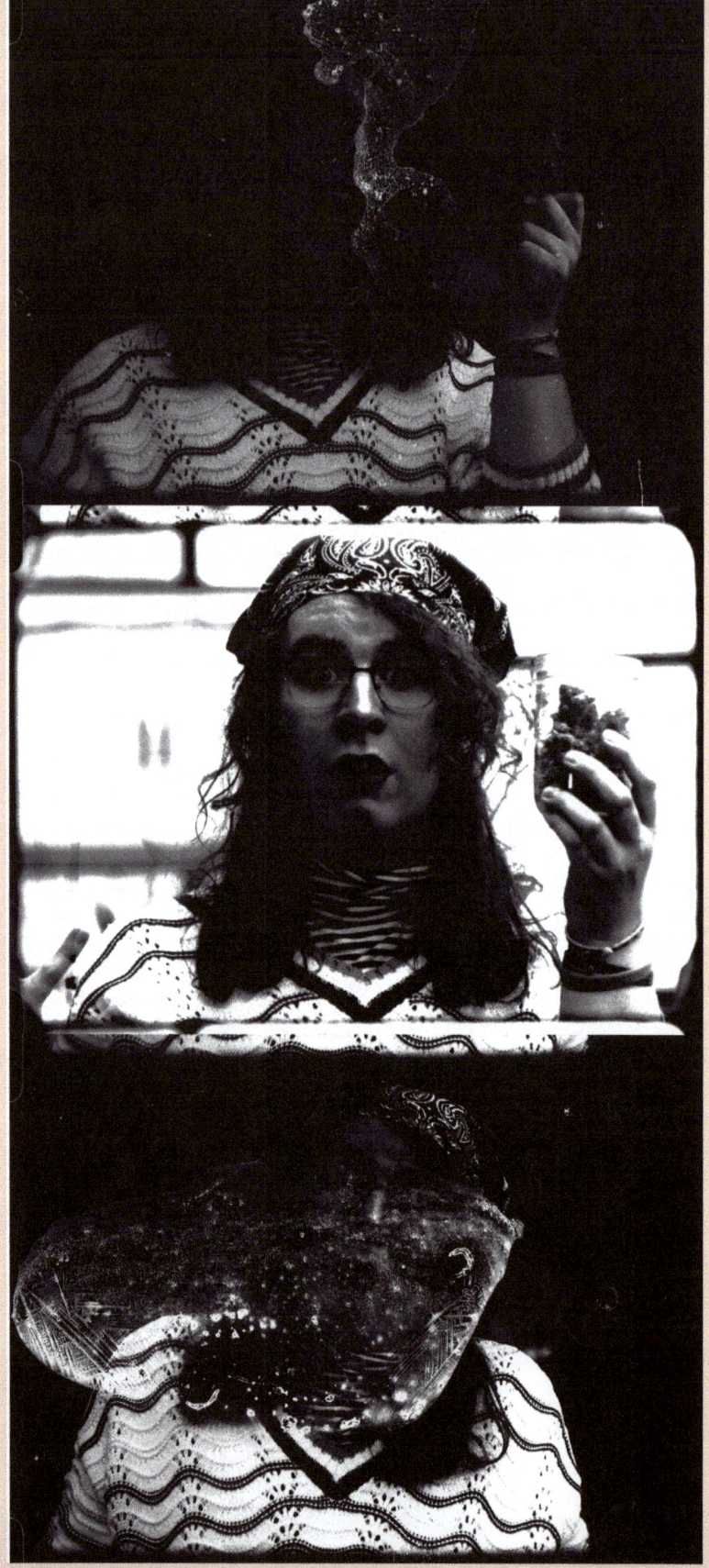

Developer C

This recipe was developed as part of a harm reduction documentary I created in the previous semester of university to showcase the versatility of the cannabis plant, and to attempt to destigmatize attitudes surrounding the drug. This work is inspired by previous plant-based developer recipes, and feels like a tongue in cheek response to global drug policy.

A very special thanks to both Michelle Trujillo and oak Grant for their help with this!

Alex Monaghan

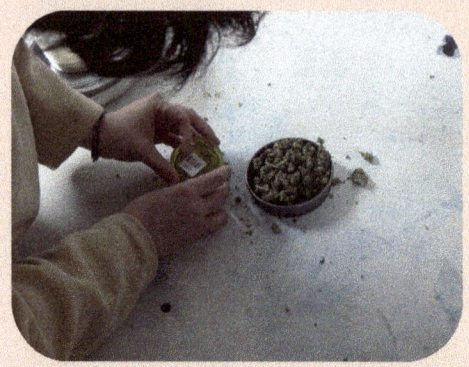

Cannabis Sativa (also known as hemp) has been grown and cultivated since the beginning of human agrarian society. From taming the animals of the land, to the waves of the sea, from being used as a dietary supplement, to even finding more recreational uses, a new use for cannabis has emerged—being used as a plant-based 16mm film developer in a student's independent study.

Cannabis is really interesting, like, super interesting. So much so in fact, that I decided to create a documentary exploring just how interesting this plant is. As a part of showcasing my fascination with this plant, and its versatility, I tried to see if I could develop a roll of Kodak Eastman 3378E in cannabis—and to my surprise I could!

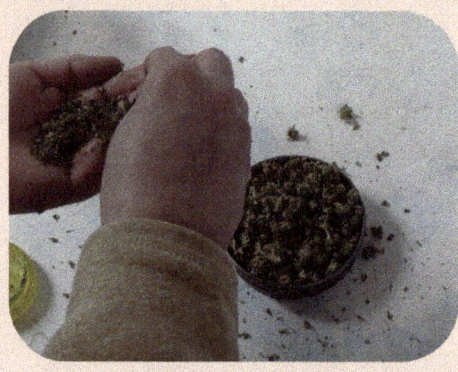

Plant based developers work due to the high polyphenolic content of a plant reacting with vitamin C powder and washing soda which allows the silver base of film to reduce and form an image. There is no hard and fast rule to say what plants may work as a developer, but the easiest way to find out which plants may work the best is if they are resinous and pungent in their appearance, just like our good friend cannabis.

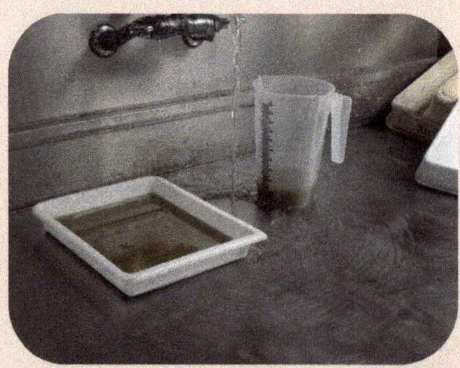

I have only made this recipe once, as it was obnoxiously expensive, but this ratio seems to work; this developer had a Ph of around 10, meaning it was very active as a developer. However, I was only able to develop around 80 feet of film, and this Developer C recipe only seemed effective for around 12 hours—the day after it produced a very faded image, even after 30 minutes of developing.

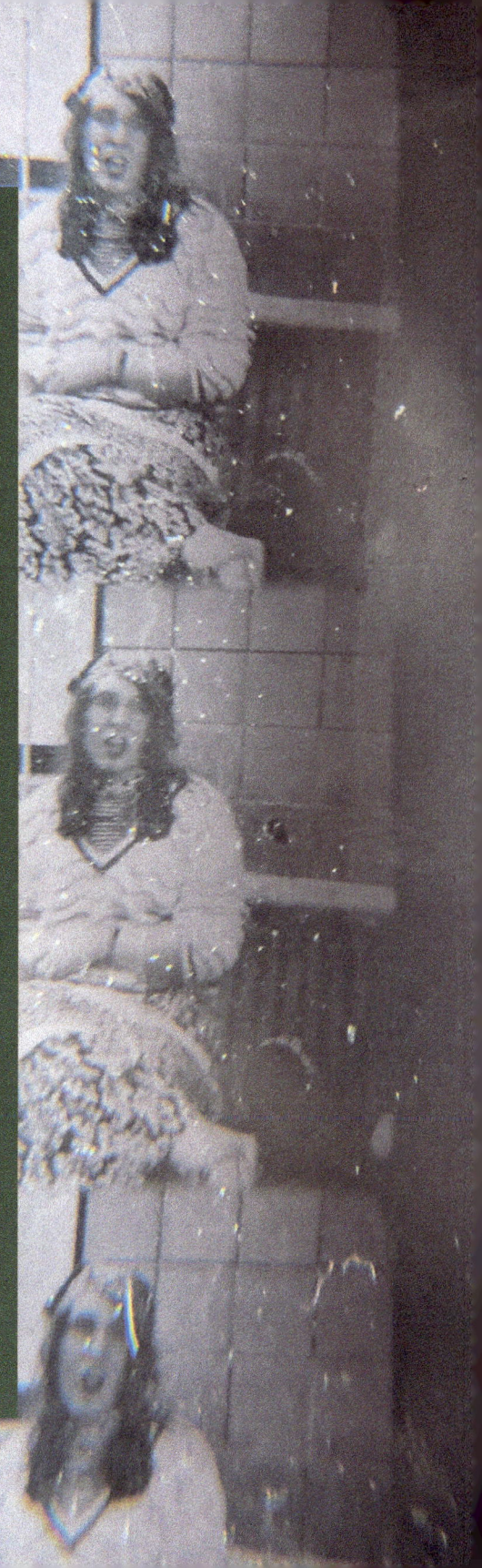

Recipe:

27g of Ground Cannabis
On/Off boil for 15 minutes in
1250 ml of Water
Leave to steep for 15 minutes
Strain with a cheesecloth
Mix Together with:
10g of Vitamin C
35g of Washing Soda

Developing:
1 minute pre-bath
Develop for 12 minutes at 35C
5 minutes stop bath
7 minutes fixer

Note: THC is not water soluble so you should NOT get a contact high. However, ground cannabis is a lung irritant, especially if aerosolized, so please wear adequate PPE when handling ground cannabis and washing soda.

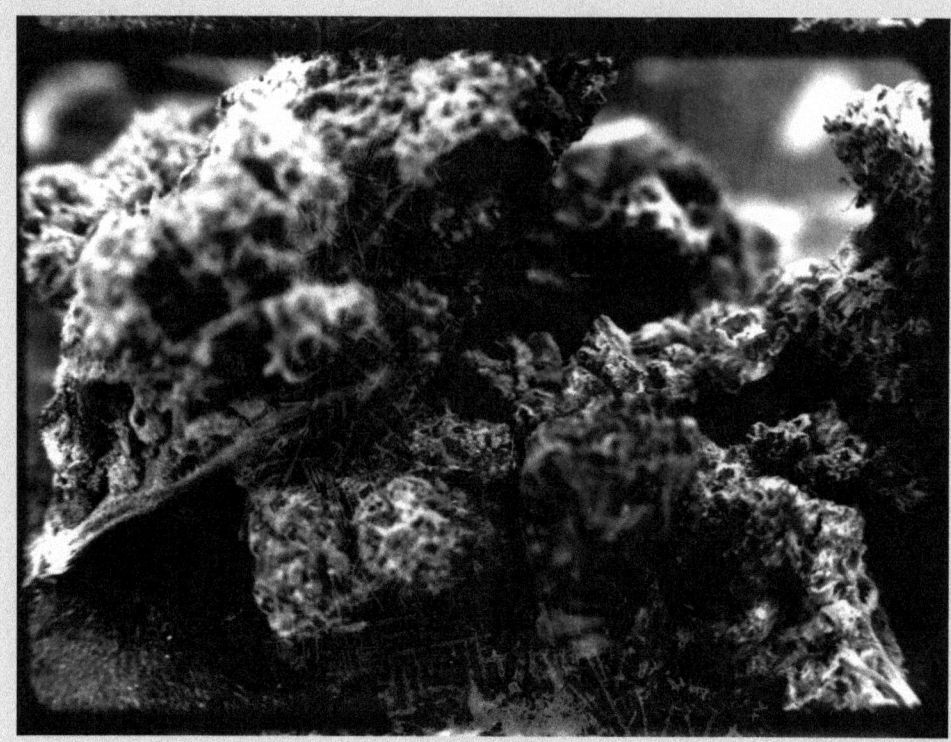

The final result yielded an image with beautiful contrast and detail–a very welcome surprise! Even as the developer started to denature, an image was nonetheless visible (despite low contrast). Someone better at image correction than myself could absolutely pull more detail out of these frames; the information is there, albeit very reduced.

An interesting feature about this developer is that a beautiful and sleek pearly resin was left on the film– even after two washes, on the earliest parts of the developed image (as a word of caution this same resinous sheen was left on everything that came in contact with the developer). More interestingly, however, was that parts of the emulsion recrystallized, leaving a beautiful hatched pattern across several frames.

No two attempts at this recipe will be the same; the cannabis I used was very old (around a year after it had been harvested), and quite dry due to the climate. There are many aspects of the cannabis plant that could influence its potency as a developer; one of it being moisture and resin content, and the other being THC percentage. Think of THC (tetrahydrocannabinol) as equivalent to ABV (Alcohol By Volume), with a higher THC percentage simply meaning a harder hitting high, due to how THC can influence resin content. Cannabis is slightly more complex than just THC percentage however, with terpenes (plant oils) influencing potency, effects, and possibly developer efficacy.

The cannabis I used had an advertised TAC (Total Active Cannabinoids, inclusive of 18.1% THC-A and 0.3% (Δ9-THC) content of 19.6 percent, however, this was more likely 16% due to its age (cannabis functions in reverse to wine, where the longer you leave it, the less potent it gets).

I posit that the moisture content, terpene content, resin content, THC percentage, and genetics all play a role in the plants efficacy as a developer, and if you plan to experiment with this more, these are the variables I encourage you to play with, especially moisture. If you're growing your own, you should experiment with drying and curing times. "Sticky" resinous cannabis is seen, at times, as more "potent," due to its "freshness" and I feel that differing resin content of the plant would absolutely play a role in the image it would help produce by either helping or hindering contrast and artifacting.

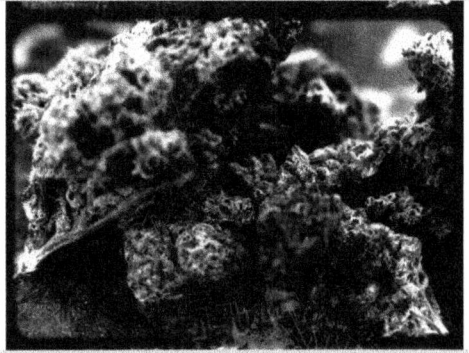

Eco-Reversal for B&W 16mm Film
(Ginkgo Leaf Developer)

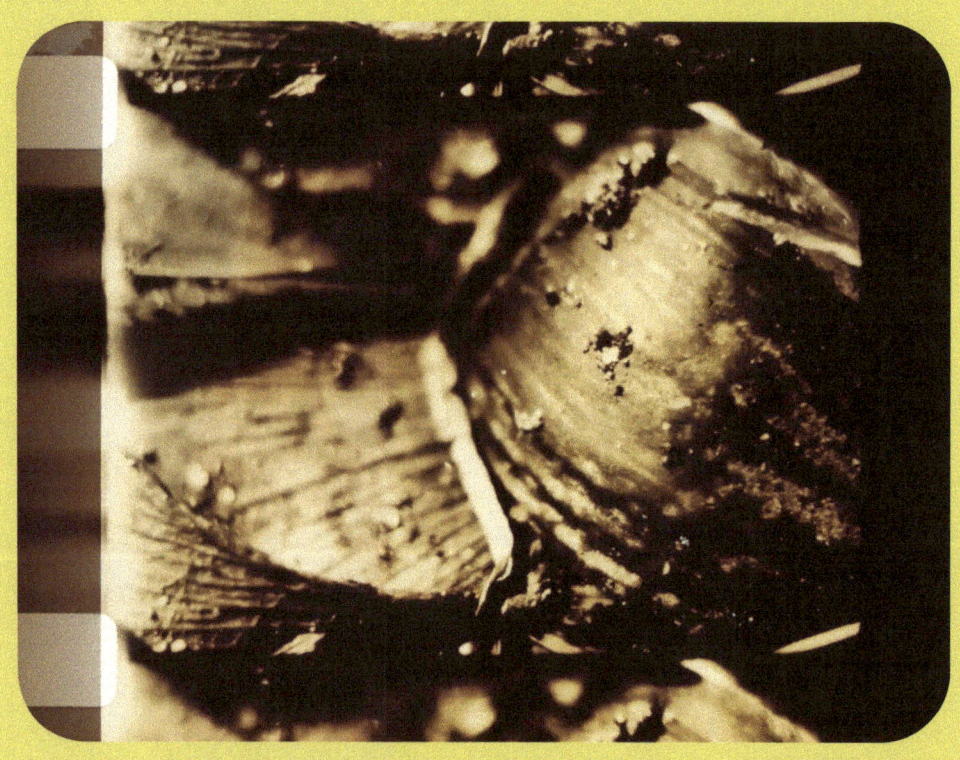

Hogan Seidel

This recipe came out of a collaboration with fellow Analog Cookbook editor Gabby Follett. That project–Objectionable Fruit–is a four-channel experimental film that uses the strange, resilient life of the ginkgo tree as a queer ecological metaphor and reflection. It combines layered Super 8, eco-processed 16mm, and phytography to explore gender fluidity, urban control, and nature's resistance to categorization.

Unlike most 16mm reversal low-waste or eco-developer recipes that still rely on traditional toxic bleach or fixer, this version keeps things fully plant-based and fixer-free–preserving the subtle toning and color shifts the ginkgo contributes. It's not technically archival, but my earliest reels (processed in early 2023) remain beautifully stable. That said, if you're after long-term stability, consider finishing your film with fixer.

Special thanks to Nick Verhaeghe, who first introduced me to using vinegar, hydrogen peroxide, and citrus in bleach steps. Check out his work!

This process prioritizes tonality, tactility, and ecological presence. It's built for experimentalists who want to work with the tonality of the plants and the unpredictability of handmade cinema. Happy processing! Send me your results!

Ingredients

This recipe yields enough chemistry for up to 200 ft of 16mm film (or up to 400 ft if you're comfortable with some beautiful chaos).

2 L water (I use tap or rain water)

50 g dried ginkgo leaves (or substitute with your favorite tea)

100 g Vitamin C powder (ascorbic acid)

200 g Washing Soda (sodium carbonate)

1600 ml Hydrogen Peroxide (12% solution- -found online or in hardware stores)

400 ml Vinegar (5% acetic acid --standard white vinegar)

1 processing tank (I use either a Lomo UPB-1 or a 900ml Paterson tank)

Changing bag or darkroom

Nitrile gloves

Reversal film stock (Kodak 3378E or Tri-X recommended)

pH strips (optional, for those who enjoy precision over chaos)

Equipment Notes

Lomo Tank: For precise and even developoing. Requires ᵕ1.5L of chemistry to fully submerge the film.

Paterson Tank: Great for chaos, uneven developing, and artifacts. You can cram 100-200 ft into one 8 reel tank. Requires ᵕ1L of chemistry.

Important: Don't pour the full 2L of developer or bleach into your tank or it will overflow.

Processing Steps

1. Make Your Developer

Boil 2 L of water. Add 50 g of dried ginkgo leaves and steep:

Hot steep: Let cool to room temp, then strain out leaves.

Cold brew: Let sit for 24-48 hours, then strain.

Add:
→ 200 g washing soda--stir until dissolved

→ 100 g vitamin C-- stir until dissolved Set aside.

2. Make Your Bleach
Wear gloves for this step.

In a separate container, combine:

→ 1600 ml hydrogen peroxide

→ 400 ml vinegar Stir gently and set aside.

3. Load Your Film

Do this in complete darkness (use a changing bag or darkroom). Wind or load your film into your tank. Choose your chaos level accordingly.

4. First Wash (Pre-Wet)

→ 1 min in room temp tap water
→ Agitate constantly
→ Drain water

NOTE: ALL CHEM IS AT ROOM TEMP (between 20-22 degrees Celsius (68-72 degrees Fahrenheit)

5. First Developer

Pour in developer

15 minutes total
→ Agitate 30 seconds at start
→ Then 10 seconds every one to two minutes

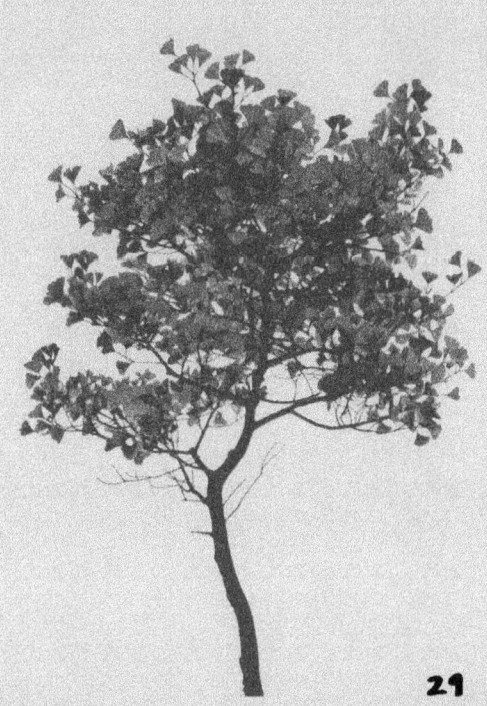

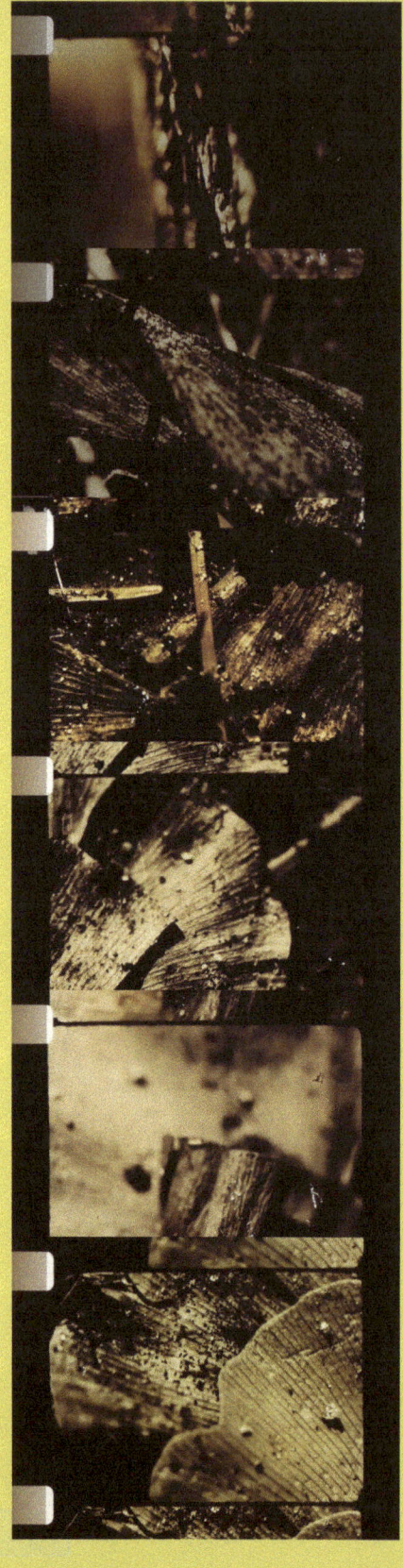

If using a Paterson tank, "burp" to release gas buildup by slightly cracking the lid

Pour developer back into a container to reuse.

6. Wash

Lomotank: Rinse with water for 2 minutes

Patterson: Fill and empty tank 3-5 times

7. Bleach

Pour in bleach solution (caution: use gloves and make sure to burp out water vapor frequently if using a closed tank)

8 minutes total
→ Agitate 30 seconds at start
→ Then 10 seconds every minute

Pour bleach back into a container to reuse.

8. Second Wash

Rinse with water for 2 minutes or fill and empty tank 3-5 times

9. Re-expose to Light

Open the tank and expose the film to room light for 2-5 minutes

If film is tangled or clumped, carefully dump it into a clean sink and rearrange

Load back into the tank

10. Second Developer

Reuse the chemistry from your first developer

15 minutes total
→ Agitate 30 seconds at start
→ Then 10 seconds every one to two minutes

Pour back into container to reuse again

11. Final Wash

Rinse film under running water for 10-15 minutes.

Hang to dry.

Notes & Variations

Substitutes: Hibiscus tea gives bluish-green tones, black tea yields sepia warmth, and beet juice creates redish-purple tones

Film stocks: High-con films like 3378E respond beautifully to this method with the least reticulation. Tri-X has a bit more chaotic, yet beautiful, results.

pH strips: Helpful if troubleshooting if using different developers. You are trying to get it to PH of 9-10. If too acidic, add more washing soda, if too basic, add more vitamin c powder.

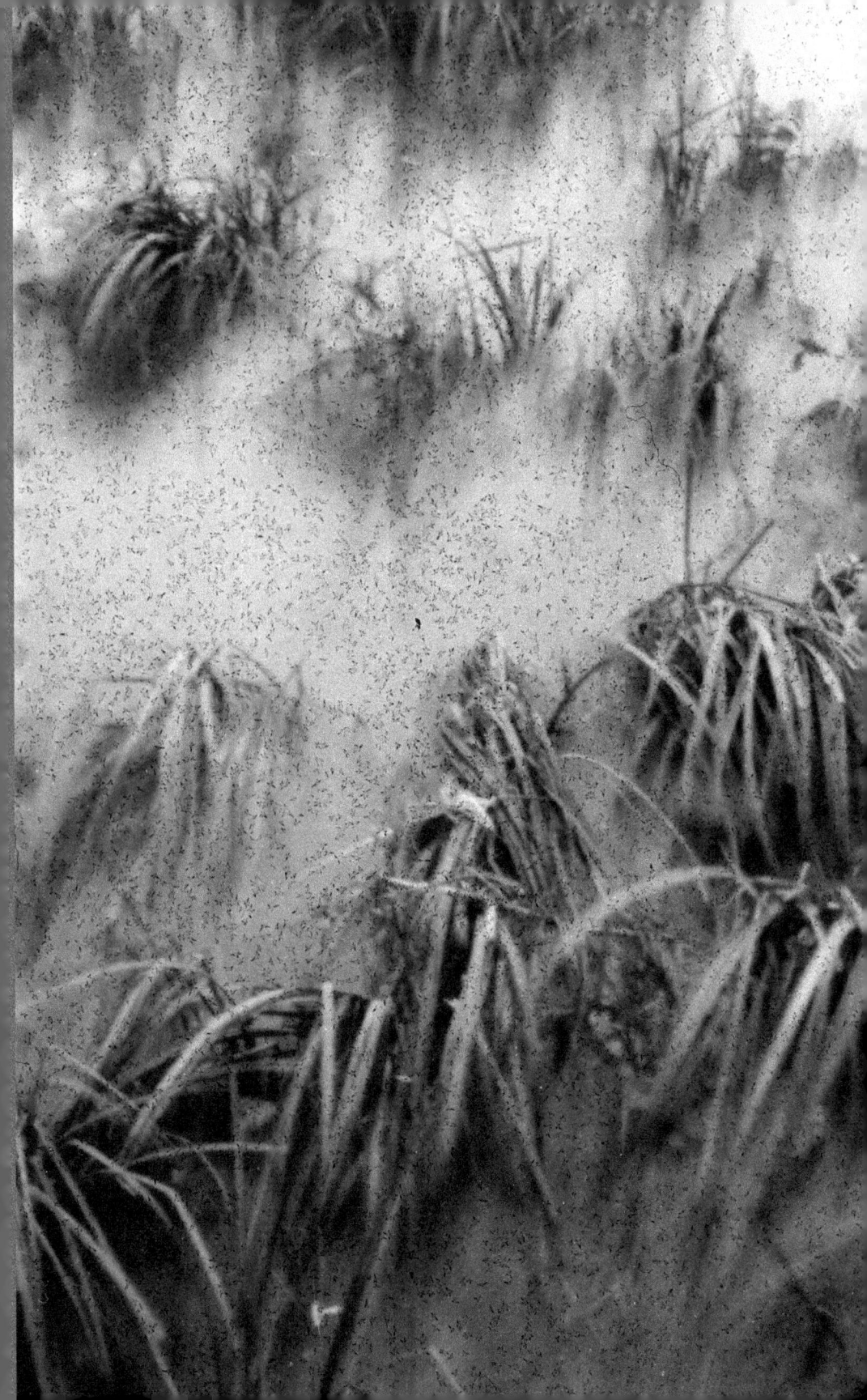

So Salty

The images are an result of my first experiment
using saltwater as a fixer for analog film in
order to make the film development process more
sustainable in additionally to using Caffenol as
a developer. After fixing the film in a saltwater
solution for 3 days, scanning in high resolution
revealed that somewhere in the process small
crystal or flower like pattern were permanently
fixed into the film. Beautiful!

As this effect has not occurred in any other film
I have developed with caffenol before I drew the
conclusion that it must be something about the
saltwater.

This error has now become a new goal and since I
have not yet been able recreate the effect, the hunt
continues.

Fabian Heller

Caffenol:

600ml of rather hard tab water
9 to 10 Tablespoons of Instant Coffee
6 to 7 Tablespoons of Soda
1 Vitamin C tablet

Eyeball and mix everything
Developed for 15 minutes, tilting the
Tank every minute

Salt Water Fixer:

One liter of water can take up around
360 grams of salt, so for 600ml equals
to 360g*0.6 =216g. But why not
make it 220g?

Leave the Film in the fixer for at least
three days. Longer is probably better,
if you got the patience.

Tilt and move the tank as often as
you schedule allows. Take the tank
with you to work or put it on your
nightstand and give it a little shake
after going to sleep each night.

When trying to recreate an error
precision must be left aside.

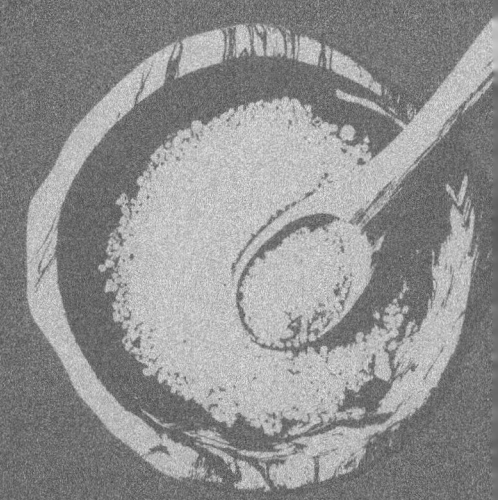

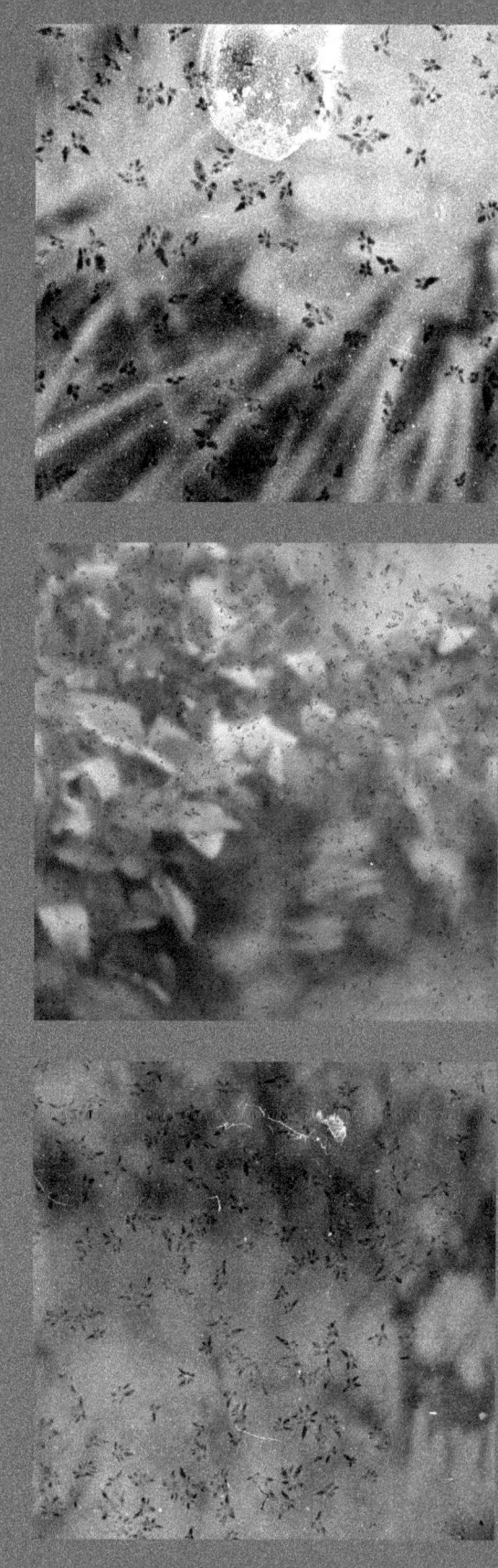

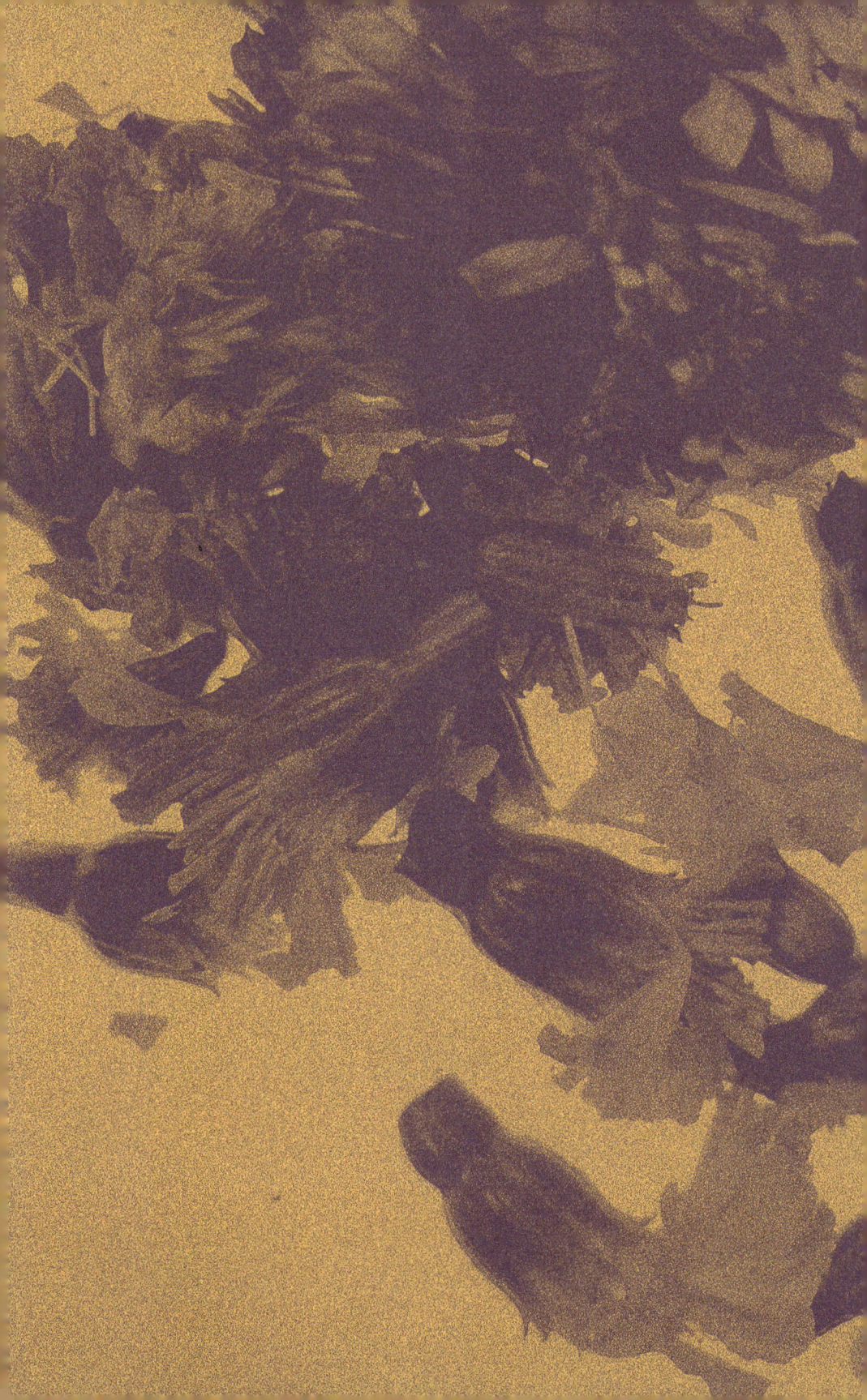

Harkat

B/W alt-developers from our Bombay neighborhood

Put together by Karan Suri Talwar, Simran Ankolkar and Namrata Sanghani of the Harkat Lab.

The Harkat lab is situated in a suburb of Bombay in an erstwhile refugee settlement. The larger area is marked by a disorganized sprinkling of pop-up shops, all selling different things. We went for a walk and picked up everything available in the vicinity. The marigold flowers came from the ladies who sit outside temples weaving fresh flowers together for prayers, the wine and beer from bottles we had only half finished (part of survival strategies within the arts in India), the coffee from an Indian estate and roses from a long lost lover. Below are our findings.The only thing missing is some of the humanity we would have brought while prepping: playing vibe music out loud and letting go of expectations is the best way to ease into making these recipes just right.

Marigold

To make developer:

350 ml Marigold extract

Add to the above:
→ 5 g Sodium Carbonate
→ 8 g Vitamin C

Developing Time: 15 min at room temp (24 °C)

Prep:

(1) 25 pieces of marigold in 350ml water, boiled for 20 min, and left overnight.

(2) Strain water from flowers and boil another 15 pieces the next day with the water from step 1. Add water to compensate for lost water through boiling.

*Don't know what boiling twice did but the solution didn't feel good to look at, so we added more flowers.

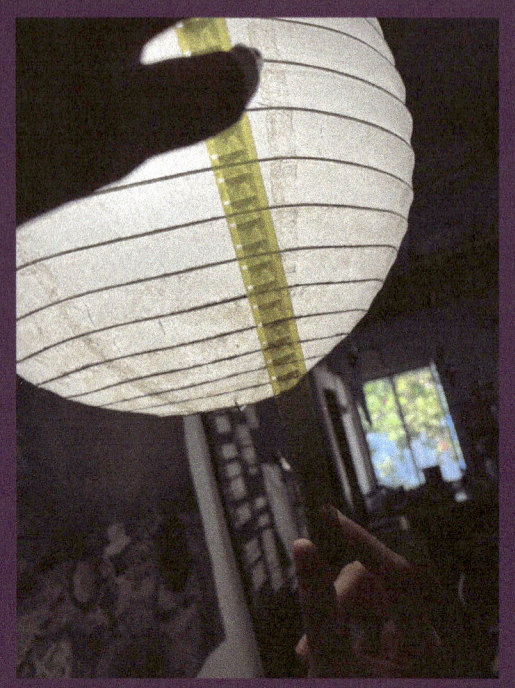

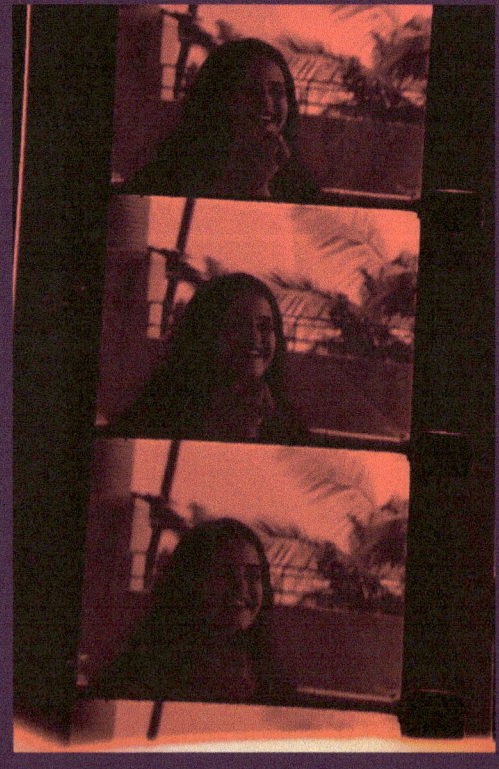

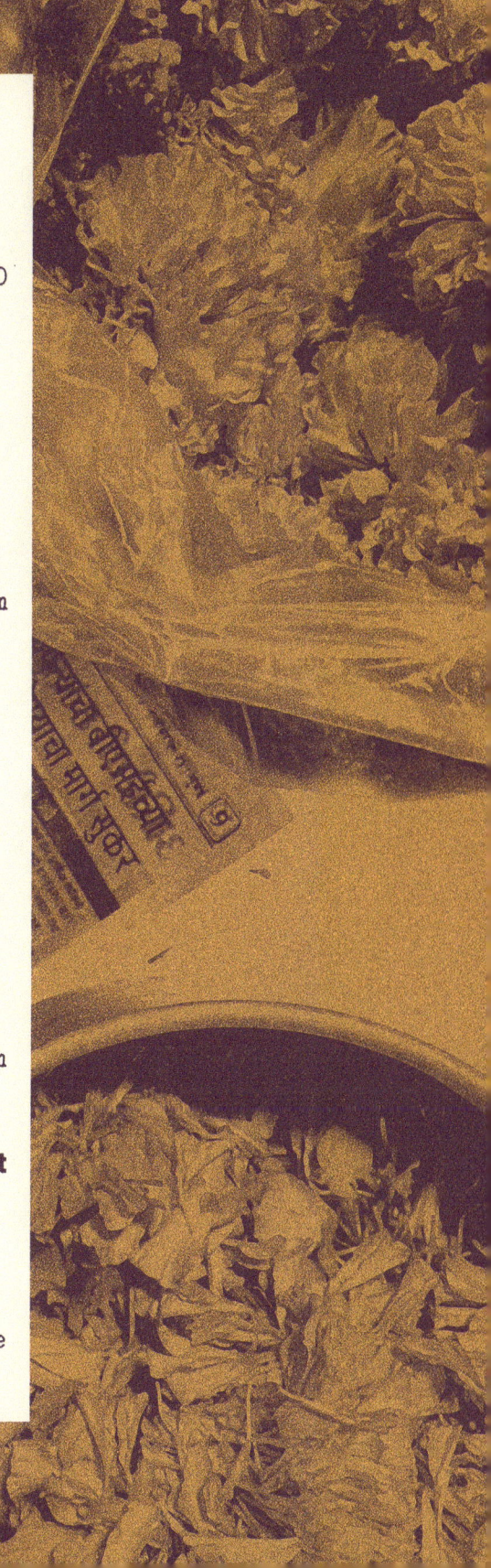

Rose

To make developer:

10 full bloom roses, boiled for 20 minutes in 350ml water

Ingredients :

→ 350 ml Rose extract
→ 10g Sodium Carbonate
→ 8 g Vitamin C

Developing Time: 12 min at room temp (24 °C)

Instant Coffee

Ingredients :

→ 5 tsp Instant Coffee
→ 3.5 tsp Sodium Carbonate
→ 3/4 tsp Vitamin C in 350ml water

Developing Time: 15 min at room temp (24 °C)

Can substitute with things found at local shop :

Sodium Carbonate→15 g Surf Excel/Ariel
Vitamin C→ 30 Vitamin C chewable tablets

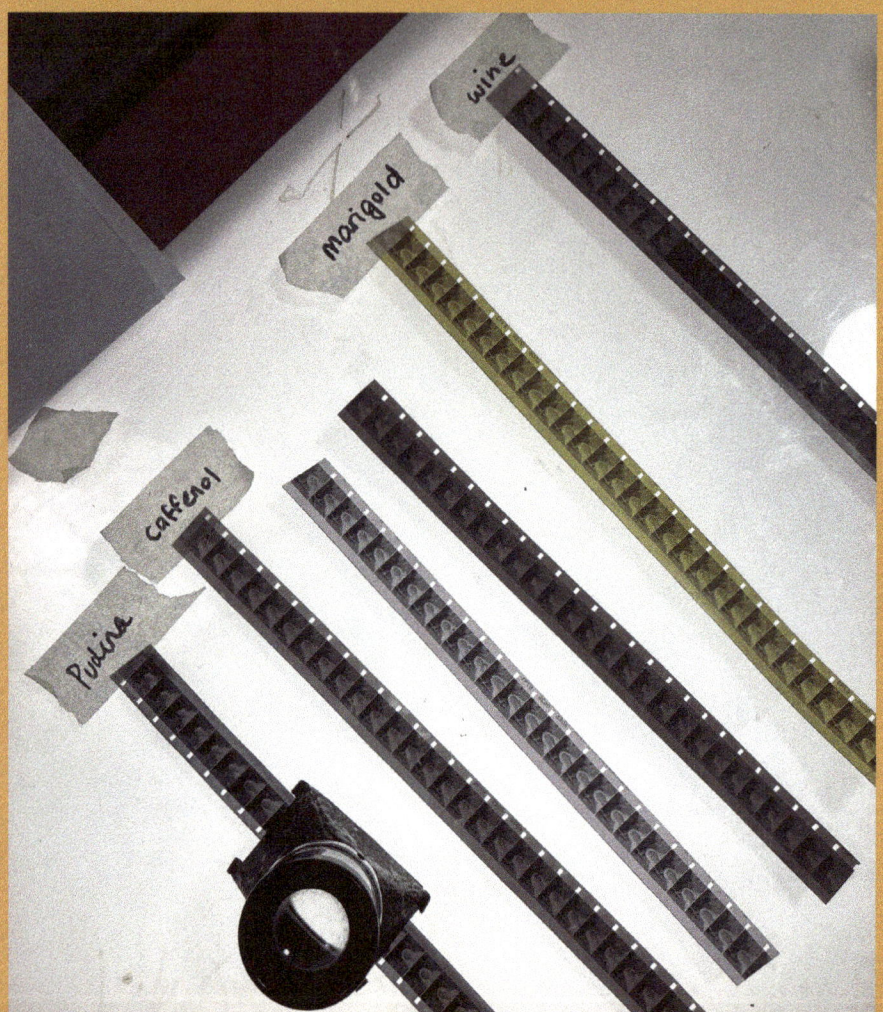

Clove

To make developer:

Boil 8 g of cloves in 300ml water, and leave overnight

Ingredients :

→300 ml Clove Solution
→30 g Sodium Carbonate
→4 g Vitamin C

Developing Time: 12 min at room temp (24 °C)

Mint

To make developer:

50 g fresh mint boiled in 600ml water boiled for 20min

Ingredients :

→600 ml Mint Solution
→10 g Washing Soda
→8 g Vitamin C

Developing Time: 15 mins at room temp (24 °C)

Port Wine

Ingredients :

→500 ml Port Wine
→15 g Sodium Carbonate
→8 g Vitamin C

Developing Time: 12 min at room temp (24 °C)

Beer

Ingredients :

→500ml beer (Bira Super Strong)
→15gms Vitamin C
→47gms Surf Excel

Developing time: 8 min at room temp (24 °C)

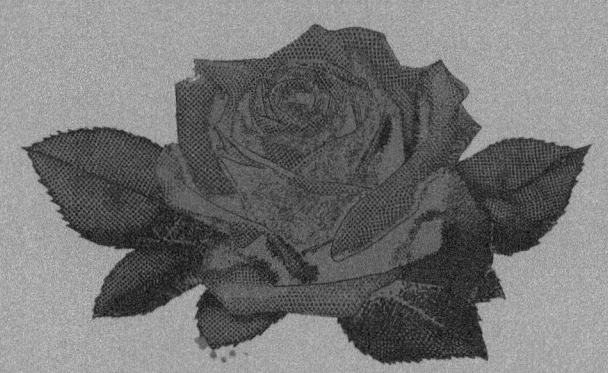

Analog Sound Recipes

Sound made with light, scratching, and laser cutting.

Nicole Blundell

Inflammatoire explores handcrafted
images and sounds on 16mm film.

This is only an example of what I
created during the workshop I taught
to guide participants.. The first part
of the exploration visually shows on
film the shape I drew (circle, line, etc)
on the sound strip 26 frames earlier
to synchronize the sound to the image.
The rest are also hand made sounds.

Inflammatoire

Voici la disposition recommandée pour le piétage noir et transparent

Here is the recommended layout for the black transparent film:leader

Élément	Position recommandée	Element	Recommended Position
Perforations	À gauche	Perforations	On the left
Côté émulsion	Vers le haut (surface mate / non brillante)	Emulsion side	Facing up (matte / non-glossy surface)
Côté base	Vers le bas (surface brillante)	Base side	Facing down (glossy surface)
Piste sonore optique	Bande étroite complètement à droite de la pellicule	Optical sound strip	Narrow band all the way to the right of the film strip
Zone image	Partie centrale, plus large	Image area	Central, wider section

Perforations à gauche, left side

Optical sound right side
Piste optique è droite

Blundell2025

Graver le son Scratching sound

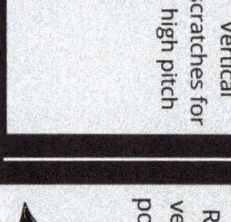

Vertical scratches for high pitch

Rayures verticales pour sons aigus

Zigzag scratches for low pitch

Zigzags pour les sons plus graves

Dots and dashes for rhythm

Points et traits pour le rhythme

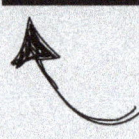
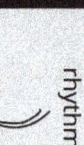
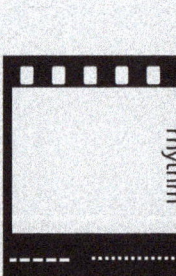

Tighter patterns for louder sounds

Motifs plus serrés pour des sons plus forts

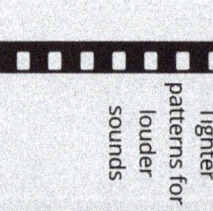

To scratch sound onto **found footage**, you must flip the film so the emulsion side is facing up. The emulsion side is duller and darker—this is where you scratch.

Pour graver du son sur une **piétage perdu**, il faut retourner la pellicule pour que le côté émulsion soit vers le haut. Le côté émulsion est plus mat et plus foncé—c'est là qu'on gratte.

Scratching sound on black or transparent leader
Graver les sons sur la pellicule noire ou transparente
16mm

Technique visuelle / Visual Technique	Effet sonore / Sound Effect	Explication / Explanation
Lignes verticales Vertical lines	**Son aigu** High-pitched tone	Fréquences rapides créées par des interruptions régulières de lumière. Fast interruptions of light create high frequencies.
Rayures en zigzag Zigzag scratches	**Son plus grave** Lower-pitched tone	Rayures moins régulières, créant une variation de fréquence. More irregular, producing deeper tones.
Points et traits Dots and dashes	**Rythme marqué** Rhythmic pattern	Chaque point = une pulsation. Dashes = rythme plus fluide ou syncopé. Each dot = a beat. Dashes = smoother or syncopated rhythm.
Motifs très serrés Very tight patterns	**Volume élevé** Louder sound	Plus il y a de détails, plus le son est fort. Denser scratching reflects more light = louder.

Blank optical sound track
Piste optique prêt à graver

DIY 16mm Optical Sound Recorder

To push a tool/technology/technique/medium to its edge and play with it, bend it, or even misuse it creatively, you first have to understand how it works. Not just on the surface, but at it's very essence: the physics, the mechanics, the logic that shaped it. Once you know that, the tool becomes open. Something you can question, adapt, or rebuild from scratch.

I first realized how optical sound works at a Klubvizija film lab workshop in about 2017 or 2018, led by Stefan Voglsinger and Guillermo Tellechea. It opened up something for me. Once I saw how sound is read off a film using a beam of light, I wondered: couldn't the same mechanism work in reverse? If a speaker is a microphone reversed, and a projector is a backwards camera, why not use a projector's sound reader to record optical sound?

Encouraged by the tutors, I started experimenting-replacing the exciter lamp with a sound modulated LED, aligning it with the sound lens and exposing film stock with audio-driven light. And it (sort of) worked! Over the next few years, I refined the system to get better sound fidelity, be simple, repeatable, and easy to build using 3D printing and accessible electronics. I developed it for the Eiki projectors as it is sort of a standard that many artist-run labs already use.

This is a small, reproducible tool that lets filmmakers strike their own optical soundtracks, without access to expensive lab equipment. It continues a long tradition of hacking the machine, understanding it, and making it do something new.

hrvoje spudic

A
film
projector's
optical sound
system has four
key parts: an exciter
lamp (A01), a sound lens
(A02), the soundtrack on
the film itself (A03) and
a photocell, often hidden
behind a sound drum (A04).

The sound lens projects a razor-thin line of light from the exciter lamp through the soundtrack onto the photocell.

As the soundtrack moves though this line of light, it modulates the light by blocking or letting it pass. Each transition from light to dark corresponds to a sound wave's phase. For example, if there are 440 black lines on 0.6ft (1 second) of film, the light flashes 440 times in a second on the photocell, and the projector speaker plays a 440Hz tone (note A4).

The soundtrack's transparent and opaque areas move steadily, encoding sound as variations in light.

— A01
— A02
— A03
— A04

The Device

This device uses the projector's steady film transport and sound lens to record sound.

By removing the exciter lamp and replacing it with an LED modulated by a sound source, it is possible to imprint sound onto unexposed film. The LED's brightness pulses with the audio signal, exposing the film's soundtrack area with variable density. Once developed, the exposed film reveals the sound as a series of dark and light lines—a variable-density optical soundtrack.

1. The modulated LED

The LED holder (B01) fits snugly over the projector's sound lens (C10). It holds

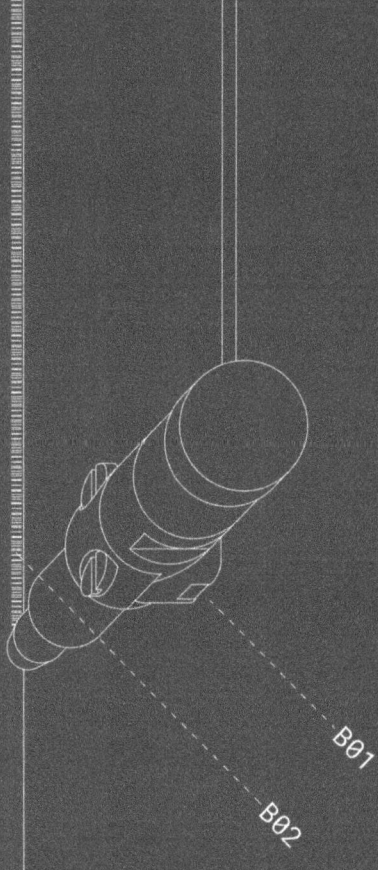

B01

B02

2. The Electronics

Audio from a sound source (laptop, phone, mixer, etc.), feeds into a basic LM386 amplifier (C12). The amplified signal oscillates between roughly –1.5V and +1.5V. A DC offset is added (C13), shifting the signal to oscillate between about 0V and +3V. This signal drives the LED: when the voltage is high, the LED is on; when low, it turns off. Sound modulates the LED brightness.

3. Light control

Once exposed and developed, the system produces a variable-density soundtrack. The frequency of the light/dark transitions corresponds to the pitch; the contrast between light and dark defines the volume.

It's important to control the maximum brightness hitting the film. This can be done electronically, but the simplest way is to place neutral density (ND) filters between the LED and the optical slit.

a white LED (C03) behind a razor-thin slit (C05) (laser-cut from thin card stock), forming a fine line of light similar to the original exciter filament.

The holder is 3D printed. SLS (Selective Laser Sintering) gives the best results and is relatively affordable, but FDM printers can also be used. It's important that the holder is opaque. The parts are assembled and clamped to the sound lens using standard M3 screws and nuts (C02, C06, C09).

The optical slit is made from a piece of black card stock (~180gsm) with a laser-cut line at the center. The gap measures between 0.2 mm and 0.3 mm. Its purpose is to mask the LED's large light spot so that the projected line of light is as narrow as possible.

Limitations

The main limitation of this system is sound sync. Accurately syncing sound to picture depends entirely on the mechanical stability of your projector. Since there's no external sync signal, any speed variation will affect timing.

One way to improve sync is to use the same projector for both the picture print and the soundtrack exposure. Another approach is to use a speed-sensing device (developed by Richard Tuohy and Diana Barrie) that reads the projector's actual speed in real time and adjusts sound playback accordingly.

Darkroom Setup and Recording

In practice, with short film lengths (like a 30 m roll), there's usually no noticeable sound drift—the projector stays accurate enough over that duration. Also, if all you want to do is add a soundtrack or narration and don't care about exact timing, this system works great!

Another drawback is that this system works best with black and white film stock. I've had partial success with color sound negatives, but the resulting soundtrack tends to be low-contrast and soft. It's still something I'm experimenting with :)

Variable-density soundtracks must be exposed and developed for maximum tonal range. This makes them much harder to copy than high-contrast variable-area tracks.

The film stock I mainly use and recommend is the beloved Orwo PF2 (rest in peace) and Kodak 3302, developed as recommended.

The most effective workflow is to first print your picture negative, rewind the print, and then strike the soundtrack directly onto it to avoid making copies.

Preparing the Eiki NT / SNT Projector:

1. Remove (NT) or disable (SNT, via fuse) the pilot lamp.
2. Optionally remove the projection lamp to avoid unwanted exposure.
3. Remove the exciter lamp (A01).
4. Mount the LED holder (B01) over the sound lens (A02) and align it perpendicular to the film path.

Striking the soundtrack:

1. Make a print of your picture negative on print film.
2. Mark a frame 5 seconds (120 frames) before picture start.
3. Rewind the print.
4. Load the print into the modified projector.
5. Advance the film until the mark aligns with the projector gate.
6. Start both the projector and the sound source simultaneously (with a 5-second silent lead-in on the audio).
7. Develop the film as usual.

Acknowledgments

This project builds on the pioneering work of Joseph Tykociński-Tykociner, whose early 1920s experiments with optical sound laid the foundation for this technique—nearly a century later, the principles remain the same. Thanks to Richard Tuohy and Diana Barrie for developing the ingenious projector sync device, and for their ongoing work in expanding the possibilities of DIY film. I'm also grateful to Matthew McWilliams for generous conversations, pointers, and support throughout the development of this project. Finally, thanks to Esther Urlus and Filmwerkplaats for hosting me in a research residency that gave space and time to push this work forward.

Test 1

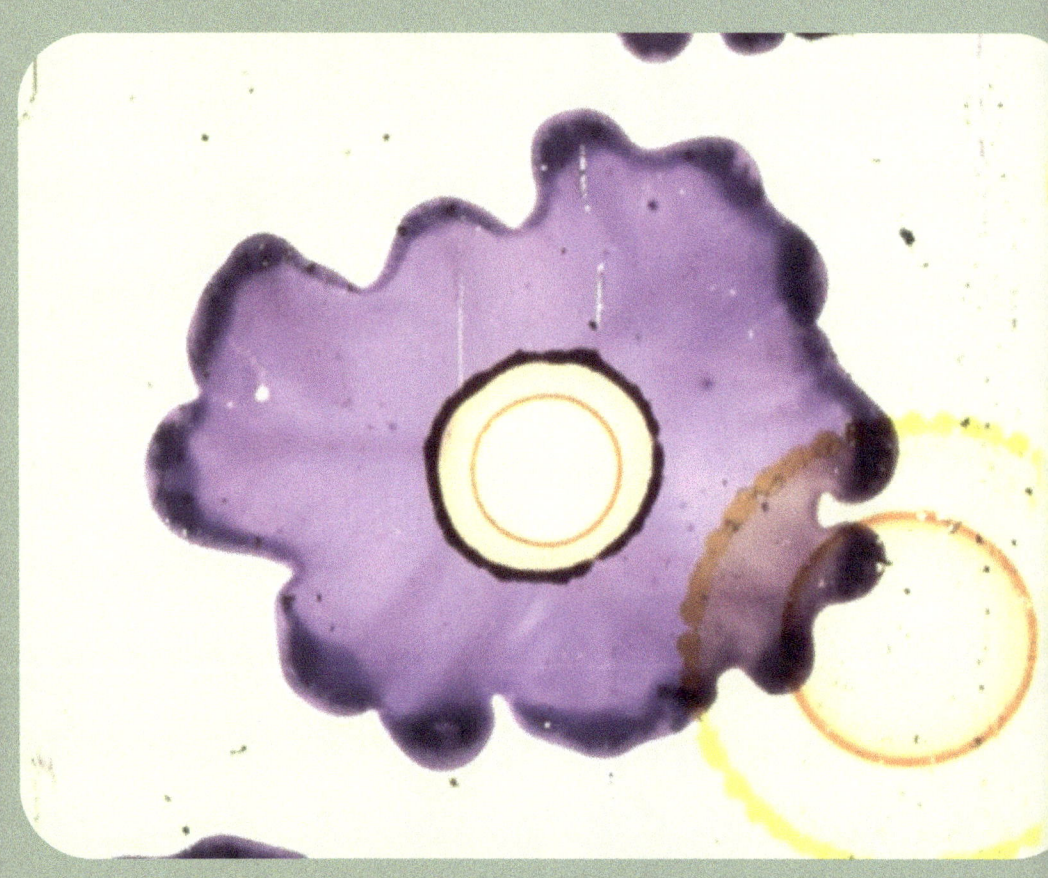

Asel Bakchakova

Test 1 is a direct animation 16mm film that is accompanied by live sound performance, where the sounds are coming from the devices that transfer light into the sound. I have several fixed sources of light (16mm projector, strobe light), but it always sounds different depending on different projectors that are used, or even the intensity of light around me, as sometimes the solar panel is able to collect the light from the surroundings. This brings film to a different level as well, changing from one projection space to another; in the end of the day it is not only a process of filmmaking but also projecting film.

As we know optical sound in analog filmmaking is basically just the light; the change in light intensity "creates" the sound. One of the ways to experiment with it is to bring this idea (sound=light) to extremes. If the sound is light, let the light actually sound. Light itself doesn't produce any sound as you can imagine. To "hear" light we need to have a device that would convert light into mechanical vibration that can be perceived as sound.

You can easily build this device. What you need for it:

→ A wire (alligator clips)
→ A speaker/headphones
→ A solar cell (solar panel)

So all you need to do is to connect a solar panel to the speaker with the wire or alligator clips.

You take a mini solar cell, take alligator clips (I advise to start with them, as they are easily removable, to see if what you are doing is actually working, and then move to soldering wire), and connect them to the panel on one end. Every solar panel has connecting points on its back, that's where you want the alligator clips to be. On the other end you connect alligator clips to your headphones or speakers by clipping them onto the stereo jack adapter. Every stereo jack has several sections on it, you want to use one clip on the top of it, and the other clip on the middle part of it. Once this is connected, you can shine different types of lights onto the panel and you will be able to hear it.

Once you are sure that the device you've built is working, you can replace alligator clips with the wire. You can take any wire or cable and solder it to the panel on one side, and to the sound cable adapter on the other side (I usually use Jack or XLR). When you have your device fixed and steady, you can connect it to the analog sound mixer (via the adapter of your choice). You can connect as many devices as you want to the separate channels of the mixer, and play with it. If you want to add some musical elements to it, you can connect a guitar pedal to the mixer and have different effects on top of your light sounds.

You can record these sounds if you want, or actually perform them live, as I did for my film Test 1.

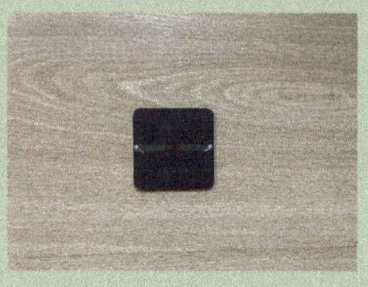

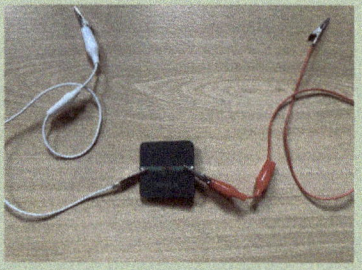

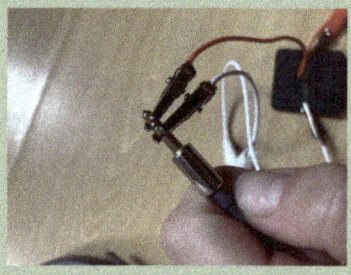

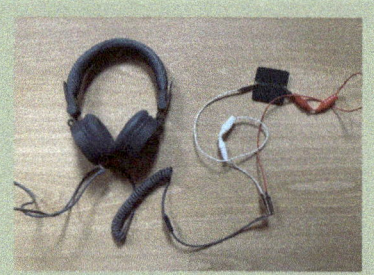

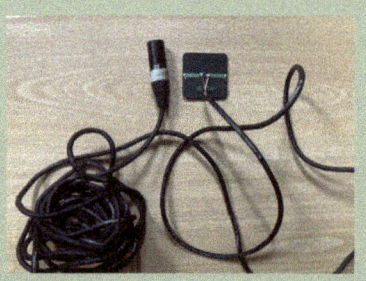

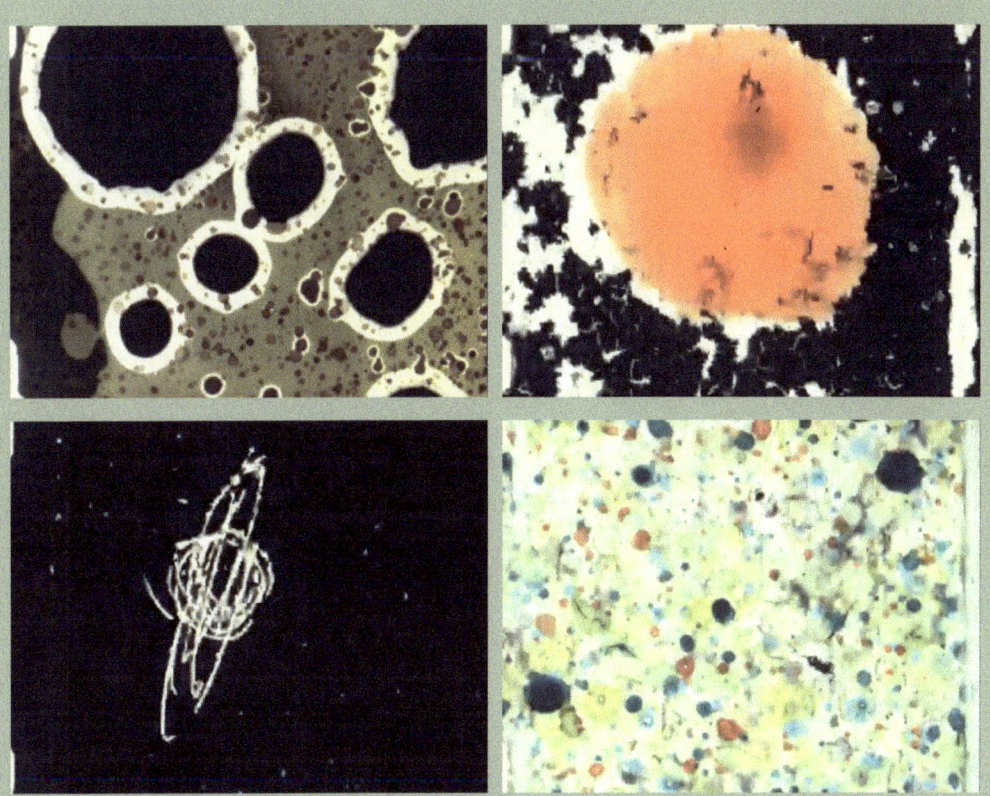

DIY Optical Soundtrack

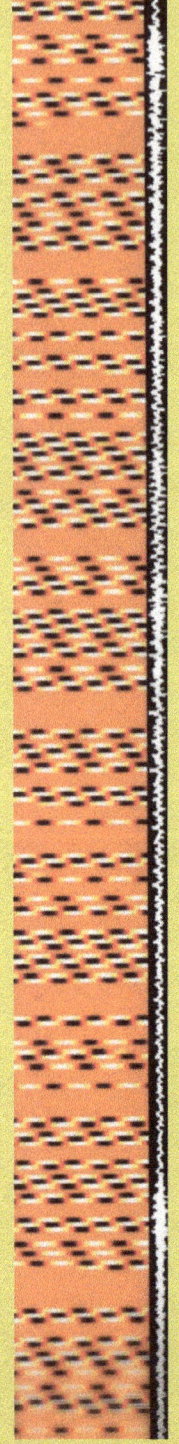

In 2023, I began a series of DIY laser engraver experiments sparked by my interest in texture, materiality, and the hands-on processes behind moving images. It all started with anthotype emulsions on Hahnemühle rag paper, which I cut, dyed, and ran through my Super 8 scanner. That early work laid the groundwork for a broader exploration into low-cost, DIY methods for working with 16mm film–especially for image duplication and optical sound.

To get around the high cost of duplicating motion-picture film, I built an Adobe Illustrator template formatted for 8.5x11" transparency paper. The template fits 11 strips of 16mm film, with 37 frames per strip, giving me around 17 seconds of footage in total. I exported each frame from my analog video piece Celestial Messages in Three Parts as .tifs and used a custom JavaScript to drop them into the right spots on the template. That script is part of the DIY Positive Print Template package (free on my website), which includes instructions on how to update the file paths if you're interested in using it yourself.

After printing the design onto transparency paper, I brought both it and the Illustrator file to a laser engraver for cutting. The process starts by etching the sprocket holes, followed by the image strips themselves to keep everything properly aligned for projection.

Once I had corrected the pitch between sprockets, I got curious— could I create an optical soundtrack to accompany these DIY prints? It turns out: yes, with some caveats. For my first test, I recorded Mary Had a Little Lamb on my phone using the Voice Memo app. Then I pulled the file into Adobe Audition and zoomed in to isolate exactly 1.54 seconds of audio (matching one film strip's duration). I took a screenshot of the waveform, brought it into Illustrator, and used Image Trace to convert it into a black-and-white graphic similar to traditional optical soundtracks. Here's where things got tricky: I forgot that most printers don't

print white. So instead of a high-contrast waveform, I ended up with just the black outline and a completely transparent center where the waveform should be. That's what caused the tinny, Edison foil-like sound in playback. Still, I consider it a successful proof of concept. I'm now experimenting with other colors—sky blue might do the trick—to improve the contrast and get more nuance in the audio.

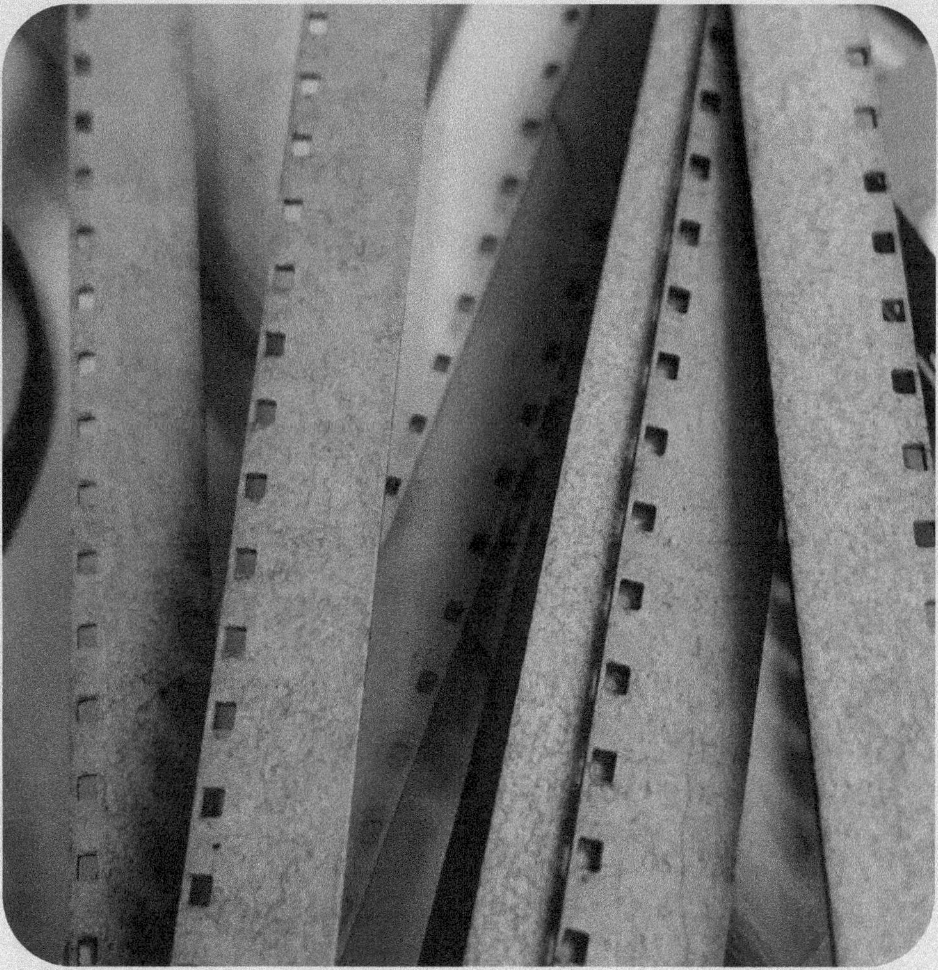

Even though there are still adjustments to make, the fact that the soundtrack plays at all feels like a win. I'd be happy to share more about the templates, techniques, or ongoing refinements with anyone interested in tinkering with this kind of analog/digital hybrid process.

Dominick Rivers

HOME PRINT MAK- ING

Cyanotype 16mm films, film soup, watergrams, and contact printing

FOR moving image maker

CYANO
-TYPE
ON
FILM:

how to prepare your film
for coating cyanotype on
it and expose image on it
under sun!

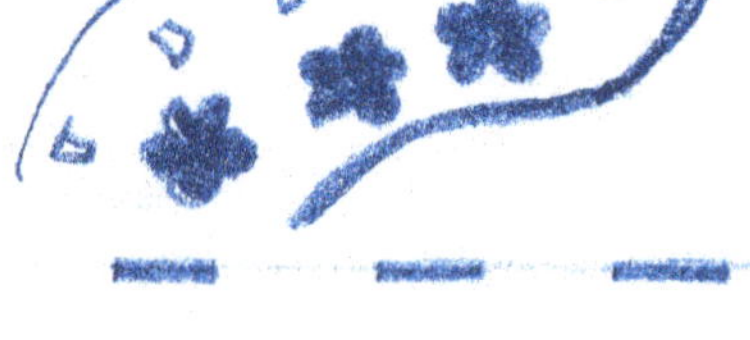

materials
&
tools:

- cyanotype solution (any brand)

  I use the liquid kit
  from photography formulary
  mix it following the
  - film *   directions!

  I use b/w hi-con film

  or expired/short end

  film, or camera film

  or print stock you can

  find that is more affordable

  16mm, 35mm, your choice

  must be undeveloped!

63

- measurement cup
- wide mouth container
- hanging rack, clips /hair dryer
- sponge brush (optional) ↗
- plastic gloves
- buckets (4L↑ prefered so the film can swim in there)
- fixer ~ 2 to 4L (any brand)
- objects or transparency printed with your desired images (negative if you want positive images, the other way around)
- big piece of glass to hold flat object or transparency in place

STEPS:

1. prepare the film

* I've heard people coat gelatin on clear leader first to let the cyanotype solution coat on the film. I haven't tried it yet, but seemed possible. The following method is to wash off the silver salt and keep the adhensive layer on the film base, so it can absorb the cyanotype solution...

1. Prepare the film - cont.

① cut the film to strips
I prefer about 4 ft long

② fill a bucket with fix
throw the film strips
in there

③ soak the film for
3-4 min until it loo
clear (agitate gently

④ Reclaim the fixer
(it's reusable)

⑤ Rinse the film for 5 m

⑥ Dry the film
(completely dried!)
Bone-dried!

2. Coat the film

method 1 — do it in a place without sunlight

① pour cyanotype solution in to a wide-mouth container

② Dip the film like the following graphic. back & forth 1-2 times

③ make sure the solution is evenly coated on film then, hang it dry

④ Dip the film in to solution again. and let it try.

⑤ store in dark box/place use it sooner the better!

method 2

① Tape the film strips in diagonal angle

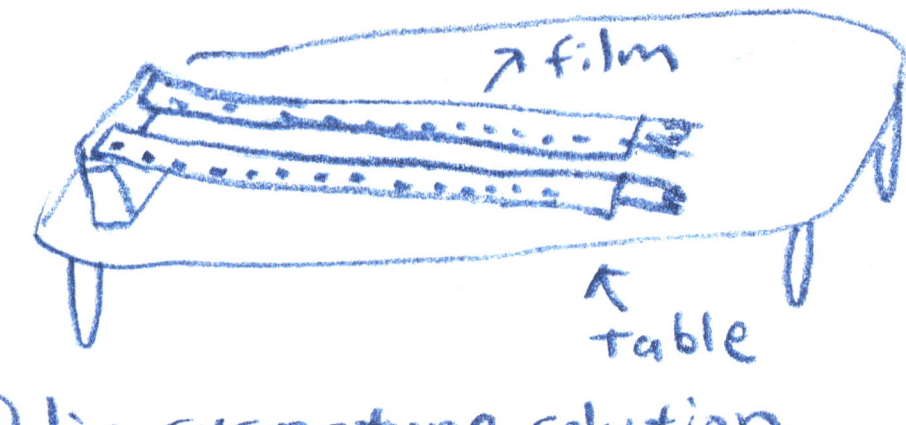

↗ film

← table

② dip cyanotype solution with a sponge brush and apply it onto film

③ coat once, let it dry

④ coat again. evenly :)

p.s. from my experience, coating twice should be enough!

☆ make sure film is completely dri... then continue to next ste...

3. EXPOSING UNDER SUN

① place your objects or transparencies
  on top of the film. secure them

✳ wait time may varies
  based on how strong the sun is.
  Usually a very bright sunlight
  takes 20-30 min.

② Observe the film strip.
  Wait till color on the edge
  of the film turns dark
  (or based on the direction
   of your cyanotype kit)

4. "Develop" or Rinse Your film

① soak your film into a bucket
  of water, gently agitate
  until the unexposed part turned
  clear (no more bleeding blue)

② hang the film dry! Enjoy the film!

(erica sheu 2025 JUNE)

Making a Cyanotype 16mm Film: *Midsummer*

In 2022, I set out to make a cyanotype film on 16mm, despite having never attempted the process before. It took about two years to complete. I worked in two makeshift darkrooms--a spare bathroom in a rental and a closet at an artist residency, as well as a traditional darkroom--spanning two states and two countries.
The result is *Midsummer*, a 3 min film, where the sunlight, along with plants, insects, and water, are all employed in the process of filmmaking. The landscape here is both material and collaborator, where its physicality is literally imprinted into the filmic surface. I began the production of the film during a month-long residency in Finland. My time in Finland coincided with Juhannus, the celebration of the longest day of the year in Finland, when the sun doesn't set.

My process was in part informed by the work of Kate Lain. While I never had the honor of attending her cyanotype workshops, her films and images served as powerful instruction in their own right. I also relied heavily on the Handmade Film Institute's webpage on cyanotype.

I hope this method builds on what those two resources have taught me and helps you create your own cyanotype film. It's a forgiving and inexpensive process, though messy and requiring quick cleanup. It's meditative and slow--the exposure depends on sunlight, which varies with the season, your location, and the weather, which I personally loved and found inspiring and fitting for my film.

Masha Vlasova,
Anna Guan

Why Cyanotype?

Many people are drawn to this process because of the resulting beautiful deep blues. And that might be enough for you. For me, I wanted to work with the filmic surface directly and to engage the film strip itself with the materiality of the landscape, where I was making the film. Because the film takes inspiration in the longest day of the year, I wanted to work with the sun directly as well. These were time- and site-specific concerns that made this the right process for Midsummer.

What You'll Need:

16mm film with emulsion

Buy it from Urbanski Film (email Larry Urbanski directly, it won't be listed online), or use unexposed film that has been fixed–this will result in clear film with emulsion.

Note: clear leader won't work because the cyanotype solution needs something to adhere to. I discuss possibilities for coating a clear leader with gelatin in notes.

Cyanotype Chemistry

You can buy chemicals from a retailer like B&H Photo and Video. They come in dry form or pre-mixed forms. I used Photographers' Formulary, INC and tried both the dry chemistry and pre-mixed options. Both work well. The Photographers' Formulary comes with clear instructions for mixing and I recommend following them. I discuss the mixing of dry chemistry below.

Darkroom trays, buckets, various water vessels of a size that will accommodate the amount of the film you're working with.

Mixing containers

These can be plastic cups, mason jars, or light tight specialized bottles and containers for photo chemistry.

Gloves

Something you might already have if you're working with chemicals or in a darkroom. Cyanotype chemistry is not very toxic but it's a good idea to protect yourself especially because this method involves handing the mixture and the film a lot.

A dark drying space

A closet, bathroom, or a darkroom with a drying cabinet (for film negatives) will work. If working at home or in another make-shift darkroom, keep in mind that the coated film strips will drip while drying, making a mess. I discuss some possible drying set ups in Notes.

Hydrogen peroxide

Use a diluted solution (1 part peroxide to 9 parts water) to intensify blues and increase contrast after washing. See the Notes section for further details.

A clean place to dry developed film strips

Time

Coating, drying, and exposing are time-consuming. I recommend setting aside several 4-hour studio sessions.

Redlight is okay because cyanotype solution is not very sensitive while wet.

Methods I used:

1. Contact Printing with Negatives

→ Requires a dark workspace. I used a university darkroom during off-hours and in the summer when the classes were out.

→ Line up negatives emulsion-to-emulsion with the film strip. Tape both to a piece of cardboard and cover with a piece of clean plexi glass.

→ Alternatively, use a contact printing frame that can be purchased at B&H or made. Be advised that contact printing frames on the B&H website are pricey and limited in size.

→Don't worry about perfect registration– misalignments can become a beautiful part of the final aesthetic.

2. Contact Printing with Positives

→ For Midsummer, I used a fading educational film showing white roses on a dark background.

→ Printing the positive on cyanotype reverses it: blue roses on a white field. It was exactly the effect I wanted.

3. Photograms (plants, insects, etc.)

→ Abstract and fast. Requires less space and no special equipment.

→ Lay materials directly on the film strip and cover with glass or plexi.

→ This was the most direct collaboration with the landscape. The plants, insects, and sunlight literally imprinted onto the film, leaving a mark.

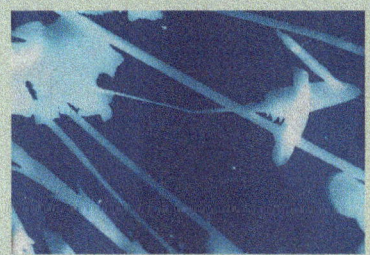
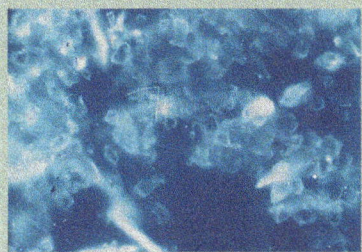
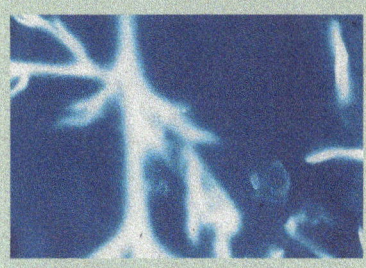
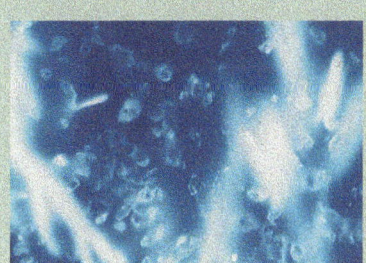

The Process

1. Pre-soak the clear film strips in water for a few hours or overnight. Then DRY it. Make sure the film strips are dry before applying cyanotype solution. The trick is to have it be recently dried. So if you're using film that you've bought somewhere (like Urbanski film), pre-soaking is essential. If you're fixing your own unexposed film, shortly before applying cyanotype, you can skip this step.

2. Mix your cyanotype solution.

Follow the instructions on your kit. You can mix from scratch using dry chemicals or use premixed parts A and B. For mixing chemistry from scratch. There are two solutions that you'll premix:

Solution A
100ml of water
25g Ferric Ammonium Citrate

Solution B100 ml of water
10g Potassium Ferricyanide

When you're ready to coat the film, mix solution A and solution B in equal parts and you're good to go!

A note on water: if mixing your own chemistry, use distilled water (although people have had good results with tap water as well.) You can try using water from a nearby lake or stream if you're going the site-specific film route–see Kate Lain's cyanotypes using water from a lake, which can be interesting and result in unexpected effects depending on what's in the water. This is where the specificity of the method can enhance your overall goals for the film!

Keep the water at room temp about 20C / 68F.

If you decide to go with the premixed option, the solutions will come in two separate light-tight bottles. Mix them in equal amounts and you're good to go!

Once mixed, the solution has a somewhat limited shelf life and will degrade (turning dim or foggy) or grow some gross slime. I've had it last a couple of weeks but have not experimented with longer periods.

If you end up with extra cyanotype solution, store it in a light tight bottle. These can be purchased at a photography store or online.

3. Coat film strips (emulsion side)

I soak strips in a tray or bucket for 2–5 minutes, then squeegee off excess with gloved fingers.

Start with short lengths, 2–3 feet. For contact printing I use 1–2 feet.

Make sure the film fits your setup (cardboard and plexi, or printing frame) and lies flat.

4. Dry the coated film

Use your chosen dark space. Drying time varies from 45 minutes in a film drying cabinet with a hot fan (common in traditional darkrooms, at universities, artists residencies with an emphasis on photography/ darkroom practices, or communal darkrooms) to 24 hours air drying.

5. Expose the film

→ **Contact Printing:** Line up your negative/positive and secure with tape. A red light is fine while working.

→ **Photograms:** Take the film outside, arrange objects on it, and cover with glass for good contact.

Exposure time varies (usually 20–35 minutes) based on sun and density of the source material. Test exposures are highly recommended (see Notes).

6. Develop

Take exposed film to your dark space and immerse it in water.

Handmade Film Institute's webpage on cyanotype recommends using two baths. It is a sensible option that helps conserve water:

→ **1st bath ("dirty")**: 3 minutes

→ **2nd bath ("clean")**: 3–10 minutes until the yellow is gone. You can also use running water on a very low setting.

Lights can come on now.

You can reuse the baths for additional development sessions. While the chemistry in cyanotype is not toxic, it's not a bad idea to dispose of the dirty bath the way you dispose of all toxic chemistry in your home or darkroom. The clean bath can go down the drain.

If you have the option, you can also leave the film under running water for ten minutes to achieve the same results.

7. Optional: Peroxide Dip

Quickly dip the film into a 1:9 hydrogen peroxide to water solution to boost the blues and contrast after the final wash. Handmade

Film Institute's webpage on cyanotype recommends this ration. You can experiment with the solution ratio too–I had to eye it a couple of times and it worked well too!

Notes

A dark drying space:

If you have access to an electric film drying cabinet, just use that, you don't need to read the rest.

Otherwise, make sure that the space where you're drying is dark or ideally light tight. If you're working in a communal darkroom at a school, you may want to work after hours so you can kill the lights because drying cabinets tend to be located in well-lit spaces, as they're intended for drying developed and fixed negatives. If you're using a communal drying cabinet, make sure to cover up as much of the inside as possible so the dripping cyanotype does not turn it blue and potentially damage other people's negatives after you're done.

If working at home, it's a good idea to plan your space and set up ahead of time. It has to be light tight. It has to accommodate the length of your film; you do not want to overlap the coated strips. This could result in poorly dried solution, weird blotches, and a bad exposure (along with a damaged negative if the wet solution gets on it)– although this could open up a space for experimentation and new discovery. One man's bad exposure, another man's material exploration! Because the coated film will drip, you will want to cover the area underneath the film with plastic or thick paper that will absorb the drips.

What I've done in the past in makeshift spaces:

→ Used push pins + a paperclip to string my coated film in a spare bathroom

→ Cloth pins holding down the film, hanging off a rope over the bathtub

→A foldable laundry drying rack and cloth pins.

Test Strip Method:

1. Expose the entire strip for 15 minutes.

2. Cover most of it, expose for 5 more minutes.

3. Slide the cover, expose the next section for 5 minutes, and repeat.

4. Develop as usual.

5. You'll get a gradient. Once dry, annotate the exposure times. Use this as a guide for future strips.

Hydrogen Peroxide:

Common concentration for Hydrogen Peroxide purchased at a drugstore is 3%. Outside the U.S., peroxide may come in higher or lower concentrations (I learned this in Finland)–so you may need to adjust accordingly.

Coating clear leader with gelatin

This year, my brilliant student Anna Guan experimented with coating glass with gelatin/cyanotype solution. Her process employed a UV nail polish lamp, which resulted in very fast exposure times. Mapping out Anna's method onto clear leader, it appears that a brush should would work well for coating. Dry and expose using the steps described above.

Here is Anna's description of the process:

Unlike watercolor paper, which readily absorbs cyanotype solution, smooth

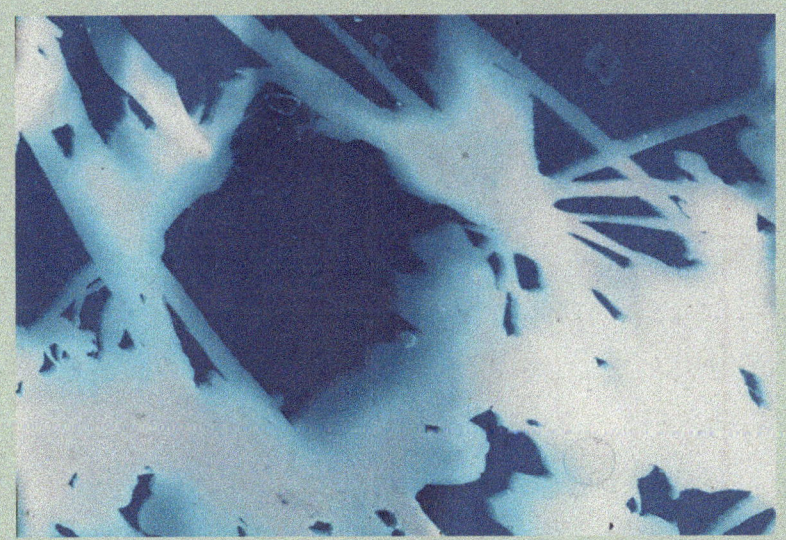

surfaces such as glass or film require a binding agent to help the solution adhere. In this process, clear, unflavored gelatin serves as the binder. To prepare the gelatin-cyanotype mixture, begin by mixing the cyanotype solution as usual. Then, place the container of solution into a pot of hot water, creating a simple water bath. The water doesn't need to boil, but it should be hot enough for small bubbles to rise. As the solution warms, gradually add gelatin and stir to combine. Precise measurements aren't required, but the mixture should have a specific viscosity: when you dip a chopstick into the liquid, a droplet should take a few seconds to fall. If the mixture is too thin, it may initially adhere to the surface but will likely wash off during the rinsing process after exposure. When coating the surface, wait until the mixture is warm to hot—comfortable enough to touch—before pouring it onto the material. Use your finger to evenly spread the liquid. While tilting the surface, as in traditional wet-plate methods, can work, it often results in a coating that's too thick, making the image harder to view unless lit very strongly. Once dry, the surface should appear matte rather than glossy. During exposure, the gelatin-cyanotype layer requires significantly less time than watercolor paper. In my experience, using a paper negative under a manicure UV lamp takes approximately 50-90 seconds; exposure time is even shorter under direct afternoon sunlight. After exposure, rinse the coated surface thoroughly until the unexposed cyanotype solution, which is typically greenish or brown in tone, has been fully washed away.

Note that a UV nail polish lamps tend to be small and might not be the best approach with clear leader. Film strips will need to lay flat for exposure. This also means that your exposure time will be longer than 50-90 seconds, likely up to 30 min. A test strip will be helpful here too.

If using a UV nail polish lamp, one could potentially exposure small sections at a time, making sure that the rest of the film is covered up and protected from a light bleed.

Testosterone Gel as Film Soup + Watergrams on Film

Avian de Keizer

Testosterone
Gel as
Film Soup

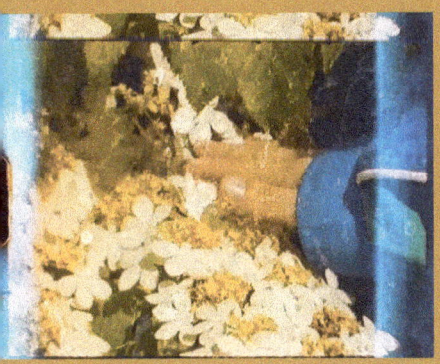

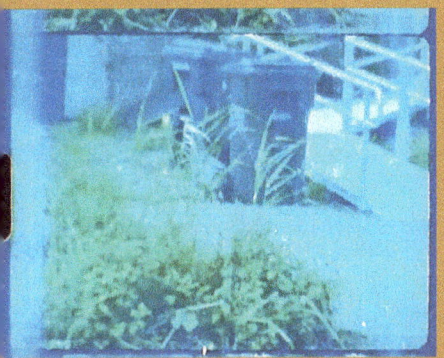

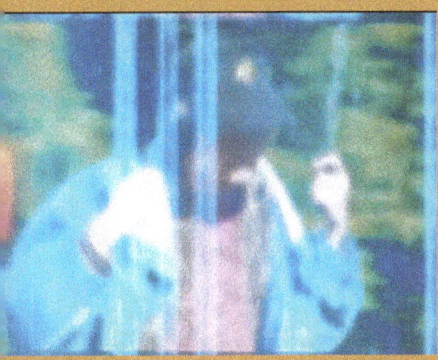

I recently film souped a Super 8 cartridge I had already shot (Kodak 200T color negative) with the medication I put on my body every single day, testosterone gel (1.62%). I soaked the cartridge in 1-2 packets (2.5-5g) of the gel, mixed with enough water to cover it completely. I weighed it down with a tiny cylinder of sour patch kids flavored gum, so that the air would slowly escape, and it would fill up. I soaked it for one and a half days. I let it dry for two days, positioned diagonally to slowly drip out excess, but got impatient and processed it after that– definitely before it was done drying. The film was wet when I pulled it out of the cartridge in the complete darkness of a changing room, and it ripped as I was pulling it out twice, which has never happened to me before. I had to break into the cartridge with nothing but a film canister opener with a pointy end, and ended up emerging victorious with film in my Patterson tank, a cut on my hand, and one absolutely destroyed cartridge.

After I processed the film (in C-41 chemistry, I know I know it's meant for ECN-2 and it ruins the chemistry but I like it), scanned it, and converted it from color negative to positive with color correction (which was much harder than I imagined it to be), I saw that the results of my film soup were some color variation around the edges and a portion of the film in the middle with a blue cast, leading into the end of the film having blue vertical stripes running across the frame. This could be from when I pulled the film out of the cartridge, if it rubbed along the rollers. I am still a bit perplexed about why it mostly affected the colors in the middle of the cartridge, though.

If I were to do it again, I would wait for it to dry for at least 10 days, as you are (kind of) supposed to do with film souped things. However, I am happy with my result, and I hope this encourages you to experiment with film soup more!

Watergrams on Film

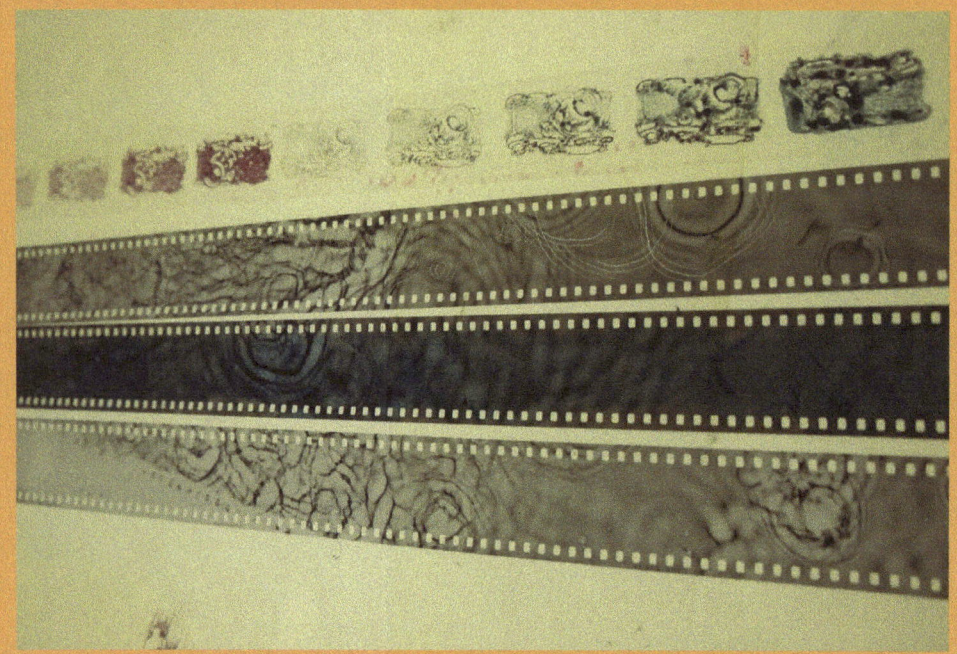

Watergrams are magical pieces of art that capture the way light refracts through rippling water. Because of the way they are made, each one you make will be completely unique. They are often done on darkroom paper, but can also be done on film and used for direct animation. While this is more unconventional, it yields even more stunning results. They can yield a wide variety of grey tones, with the possibility for deep blacks in the strong ripples and complete transparency between them. They are captured across the whole film, sprockets included, and can be used for optical sound in addition to direct animation. After this process, you will be left with an awe-inspiring physical object to hold and a new medium to add to your toolkit.

What you will need:

→ Access to a darkroom (red lights only, no yellow!!) with no one else around. You will be firing a flash in the darkroom, which will fog others' work

→ Darkroom tray (as small or as big as you like)

→ Water

→ Water jug for pouring

→ Camera flash: separate from a camera, preferably (an old film camera flash works)

→ Diffusion for the flash: filters, medical masks, gloves, anything you can find and reuse)

→ Photosensitive film stock: low ISO sound recording stocks work best, and it should be orthochromatic (Kodak 3378E works wonderfully)

→ One assistant to pour the water or fire the flash (optional but sometimes necessary)

→ Developer, stop, fixer: I have used the darkroom's paper chemistry for this before, and it has worked well.

Process:

1. Set up your tray filled with at least 1 inch of water

2. Cut a strip of film and submerge it in the water in the darkroom tray

3. Cover your flash with some light diffusion to start (2 medical masks/3 gloves/1 filter if you need extra guidance)

4. Pour the water into the tray to cause ripples and fire the flash from above the tray

5. Develop, stop, and fix the film (as per the darkroom/chemistry's recommendations) and take a look at it in the light - is it a watergram? Is it blank? Is it completely black?

6. Adjust your process accordingly and repeat

→If it was blank, you need brighter light. Take some diffusion off or stand closer to the tray

→If it was black or too dark, you need less light. Add more layers of diffusion or stand farther away from the tray

There is a lot of flexibility in this process to play with the results and outcomes. You can do batches with many strips at the same time, but I would only recommend this after you have the exposure nailed down, and you may get some overlap of the film as it floats, resulting in some sprocket holes (but who doesn't love those) and blank spots (more to fill in later)! Some may prefer darker watergrams, some lighter. You can play around with how much water is in the tray and how the water is poured. You can also place objects on top of the film, such as flowers, and make a combination of a watergram and a photogram at the same time. The possibilities are endless!

I love the look of these so much, I have been thinking about getting a tattoo of a watergram film strip. I have to find an artist who will do that complicated design and shading, though. Let me know if you know anyone or have any ideas, and please share what you create with your watergrams! aviandphotography@gmail.com

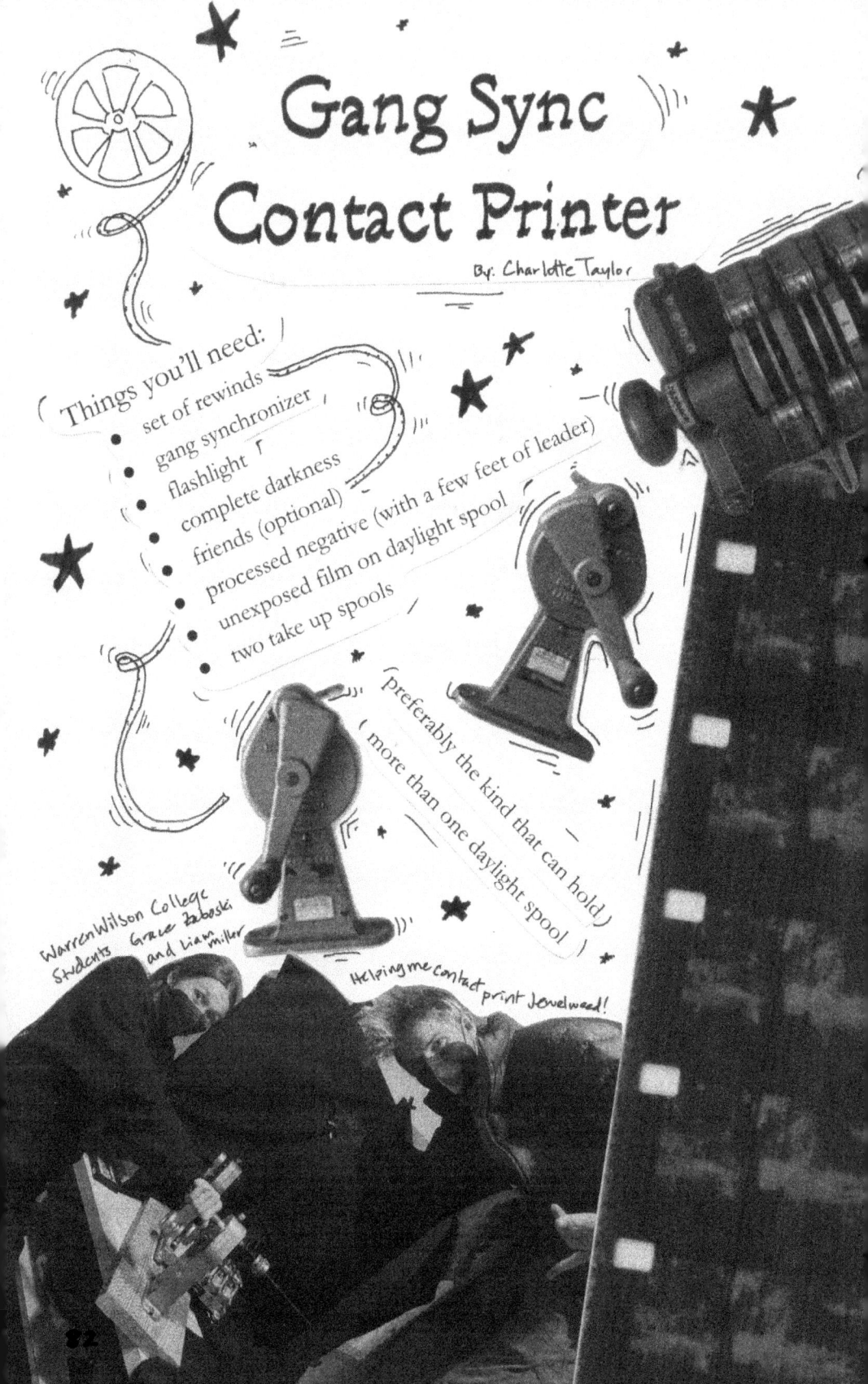

Gang Sync Contact Printer

By: Charlotte Taylor

Things you'll need:

- set of rewinds
- gang synchronizer
- flashlight
- complete darkness
- friends (optional)
- processed negative (with a few feet of leader)
- unexposed film on daylight spool
- two take up spools

preferably the kind that can hold more than one daylight spool

Warren Wilson College Students Grace Zaboski and Liam Miller

Helping me contact print Jewelweed!

Steps:

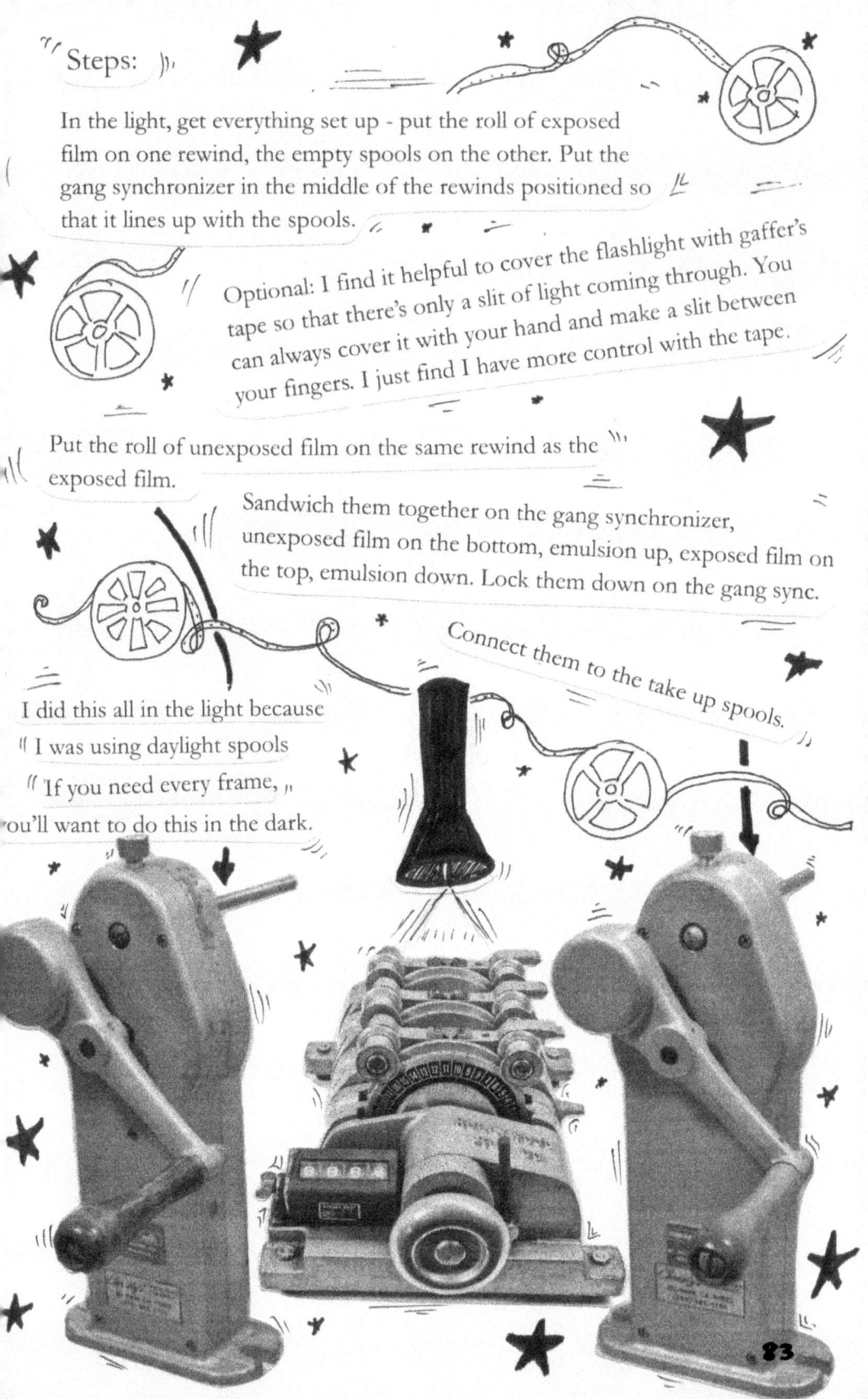

In the light, get everything set up - put the roll of exposed film on one rewind, the empty spools on the other. Put the gang synchronizer in the middle of the rewinds positioned so that it lines up with the spools.

Optional: I find it helpful to cover the flashlight with gaffer's tape so that there's only a slit of light coming through. You can always cover it with your hand and make a slit between your fingers. I just find I have more control with the tape.

Put the roll of unexposed film on the same rewind as the exposed film.

Sandwich them together on the gang synchronizer, unexposed film on the bottom, emulsion up, exposed film on the top, emulsion down. Lock them down on the gang sync.

Connect them to the take up spools.

I did this all in the light because I was using daylight spools. If you need every frame, you'll want to do this in the dark.

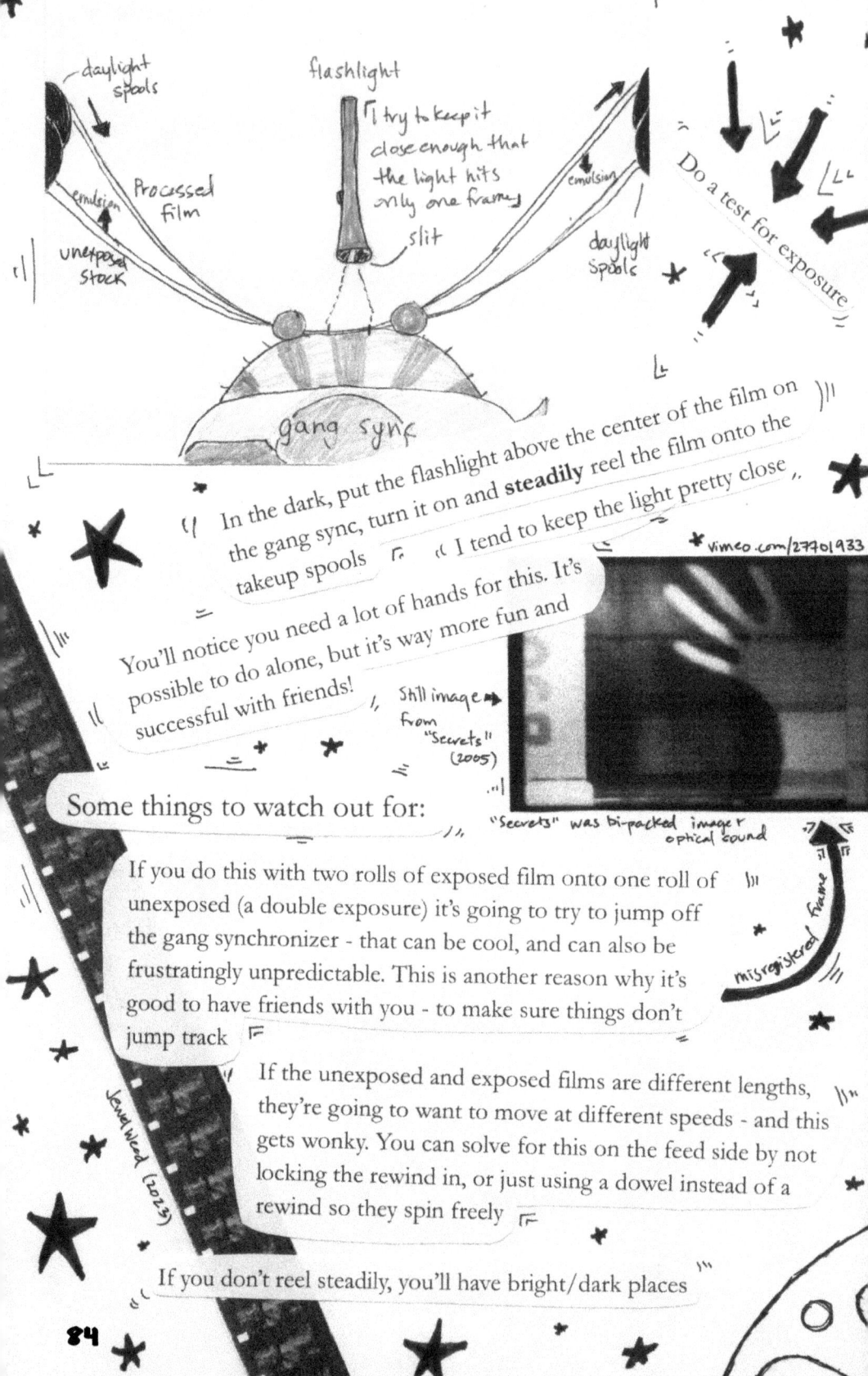

daylight spools

flashlight

"I try to keep it close enough that the light hits only one frame slit"

emulsion

Processed Film

emulsion

daylight spools

unexposed stock

Do a test for exposure

gang sync

In the dark, put the flashlight above the center of the film on the gang sync, turn it on and **steadily** reel the film onto the takeup spools   I tend to keep the light pretty close

You'll notice you need a lot of hands for this. It's possible to do alone, but it's way more fun and successful with friends!

* vimeo.com/27701933

Still image from "Secrets" (2005)

"Secrets" was bi-packed image + optical sound

Some things to watch out for:

If you do this with two rolls of exposed film onto one roll of unexposed (a double exposure) it's going to try to jump off the gang synchronizer - that can be cool, and can also be frustratingly unpredictable. This is another reason why it's good to have friends with you - to make sure things don't jump track

misregistered frame

If the unexposed and exposed films are different lengths, they're going to want to move at different speeds - and this gets wonky. You can solve for this on the feed side by not locking the rewind in, or just using a dowel instead of a rewind so they spin freely

Jewelweed (2023)

If you don't reel steadily, you'll have bright/dark places

84

Some things to play with:

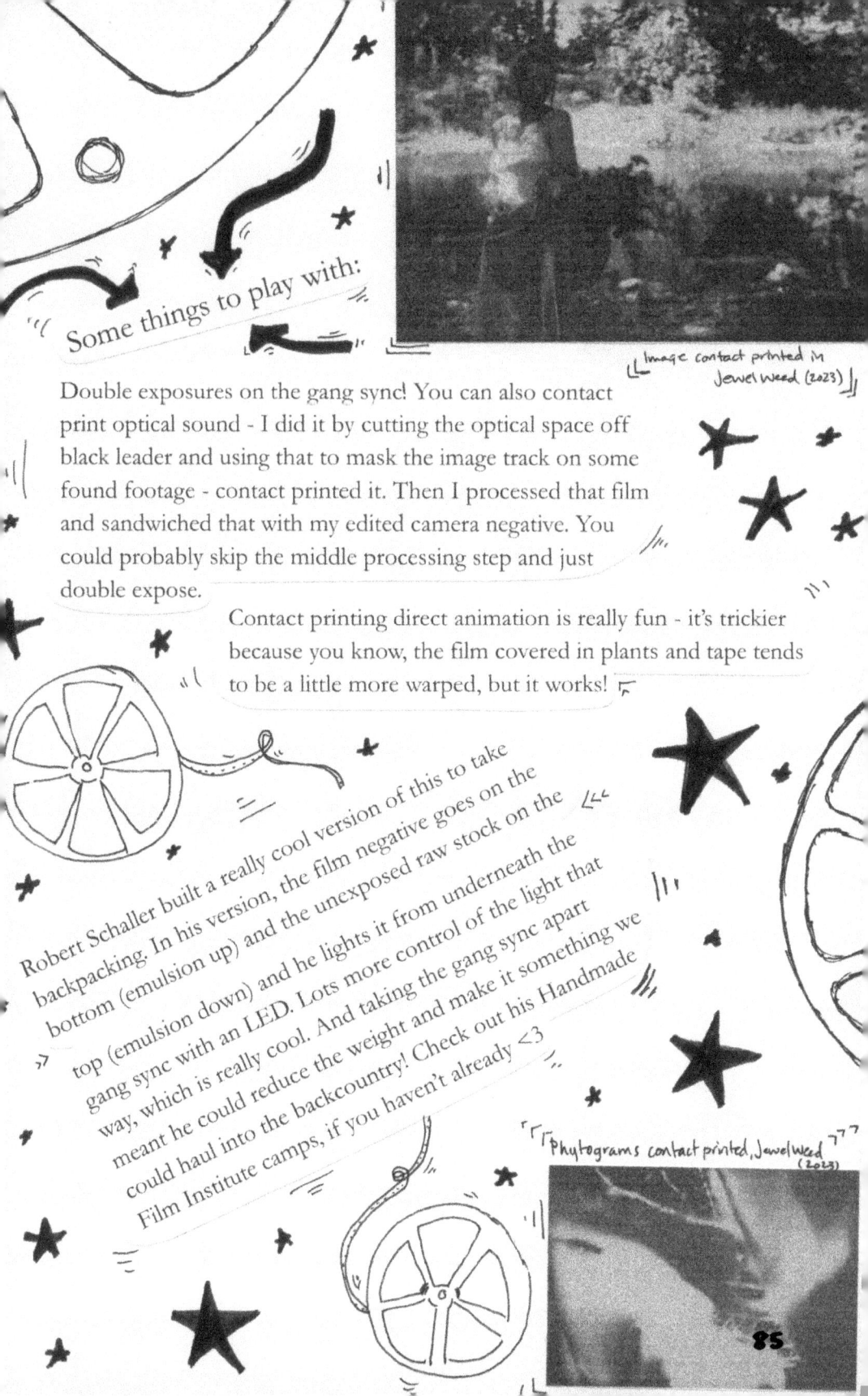

Image contact printed in Jewelweed (2023)

Double exposures on the gang sync! You can also contact print optical sound - I did it by cutting the optical space off black leader and using that to mask the image track on some found footage - contact printed it. Then I processed that film and sandwiched that with my edited camera negative. You could probably skip the middle processing step and just double expose.

Contact printing direct animation is really fun - it's trickier because you know, the film covered in plants and tape tends to be a little more warped, but it works!

Robert Schaller built a really cool version of this to take backpacking. In his version, the film negative goes on the bottom (emulsion up) and the unexposed raw stock on the top (emulsion down) and he lights it from underneath the gang sync with an LED. Lots more control of the light that way, which is really cool. And taking the gang sync apart meant he could reduce the weight and make it something we could haul into the backcountry! Check out his Handmade Film Institute camps, if you haven't already <3

Phytograms contact printed, Jewelweed (2023)

85

playing with Process

Playing with emulsion, solarization, double exposures, fabric and a piano.

Pseudo-Solarization Recipe

By MaLo Sutra Fish

Malo Sutra Fish.

Tri-X Reversal Film _ Pseudo Solarization.

This is a recipe for pseudo-solarization effect done during film processing.

Film processing used: C4.

1st bath: D94 → this is where it
2nd bath: R9   happens.
3rd bath: CB2
4th bath: D95

You'll need a small flashlight, preferably a pocket-size one that you can easily click on & off. You need to mimick flash type of lighting effect.

If you use lomo tanks, make sure to do this with the lid off in total darkness.

Think of your processing time in thirds, while visualizing the curve graph used to depict film dynamics.
This is going to help you aim the correct flashing time for the effect you want.

Maho Sutra Fish

- First third: the image is at the first stage of processing, meaning the chemicals nearly had time to have any effect on the film.
  └→ if you flash during this time you will burn your image, creating a white / transparency effect.

- Second third: this is the optimal window for solarization as the film has had enough exposure to chemicals allowing for silver agents to be partially processed yet remaining active. Your effect will efficiently impact the image's mid-tones.

- Third third: this is the last portion of processing. Flashing during this time will have a fog like effect on film rather than a "negative" like effect, as the chemicals have almost finished processing the film.

→ · Depending on what you wished for you can play with these "solarization" portions

Malo Sutra Fish

Another thing to consider is the distance from the flashlight to the film, as well as amount of light intensity.

↳ . the closer you are, the narrower is the light ray, but also the more intense. → more likely to burn

. the farther the flashlight is, the wider & softer the light ray will be. → more likely to fog.

Last but not least, if you are using a reel; your film is therefore standing perpendicularly as well as lined up.

Giving an angle to the flashlight will ensure a better cover of light.

Note this is just to depict angle, NOT intensity.

With this type of set-up, you will have a sense of directional light.

→ Also, if you film is lined up the light ray is going to be filtered by the film. This is going to produce a dimmer solarisation effect onto the photograms as well as casting shadows, especially sprocket holes.

→ As your film is reeled in a spiral, you're also going to have a rhythm of solarized vs unsolarized images

If you wish to isolate your effect, you should consider selecting the portion of film you want to solarize.
Cut portions of about 2 feet / 1 meter long and use the bottle method.

The bottle method is a trick used notably by French filmmaker Gaëlle Rouard who specializes in chemical and pseudo solarisation effects. She usually uses print film which is less sensitive to light - therefore needing longer flashes during a pseudo solarisation process.

Malo Sutra Fish

Bottle Method:

. Take a plastic or glass bottle.
. Pour in the developper.
. tape your film together to create
a loop. Or leave it as is.
  perks of loop: less likely to slip
  at bottom of bottle.
  cons of loop: harder to gage start
  vs end of your film segment.

→ Dip in your film for the 1/3 of
time making sure you "circulate"
evenly film in chemicals.

→ 2/3 of time: extend film out of
  bottle as much as possible and
  flash it according to will
    NB: I would prefer a certain
    distance to avoid total burn

→ Resume processing circulating film
in & out of bottle opening for remaing
of time.

NB: this method needs several
  adjustment tests.   13

Malo Sutra Fish

I've used the reel method directly
onto my Super 8 TriX reversal film.
I had 3 reels + 1 spaghetti trial.
I solarized two.

1st reel: 1/3 window with angle,
    targeting 1/4 of reel
    lesser than 2ft away, but
    definitely over 1 foot.

2nd reel: 2/3 window, closer
    narrow flash bouncing off the
    steel of my tank.

→ Yes, indeed, if you use steel tank
you can play with light reflection

I did it twice in opposite

3rd → Spaghetti dump solarized 2 minutes
    in out of a six minute process
ORWO   3 flashes, are bouncing off
film   the tank walls.

15 ft in reel: chemical solarisation for
    which I omitted R9 bath.

Malo Sutra Fish

The results of this can be seen in
my music film done for FLAT WORMS.

↳ Flat worms - See You At The Show
   official music video.

   ↳ Shot on Kodak TriX + Orwo UN54
      pushed 2 steps   pushed 3 steps

Camera used: CANON 814 AZ.

Processed at L'Etna Lab - Montreuil

C4 temp. 22.5°C

Stainless steel open tank method.

FiLM EMULSioN LiFT

by Amelia Mevers

Step 1

cut your film into managable strips! too long and this becomes a pain later.

Step 2

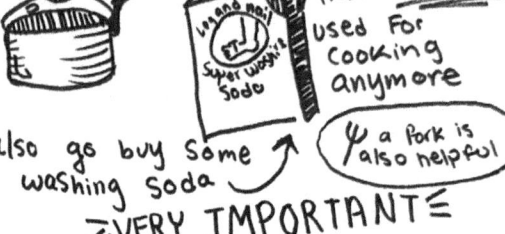

Find (or thrift) an old pot that **IS NOT** used for cooking anymore

also go buy some washing soda ⇒ VERY IMPORTANTE

(⊌ a fork is also helpful)

Step 3

time to become a mad scientist

Super cool and hot

↓ ding!

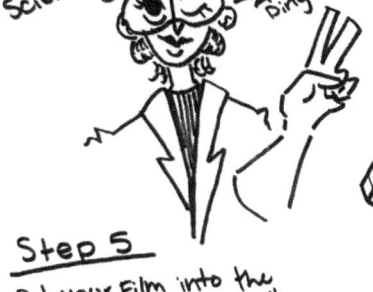

Step 4

Fill your pot with water and add washing soda and bring to a rolling boil.

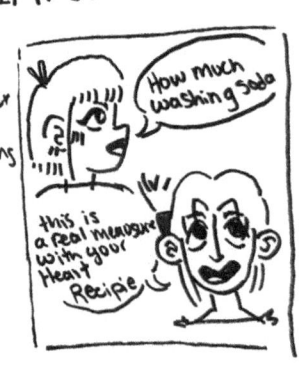

How much washing soda

this is a real measure with your Heart Recipe

Step 5

Put your film into the pot and leave untill you can see emulsion start to lift off the strips

30 sec to 1 min

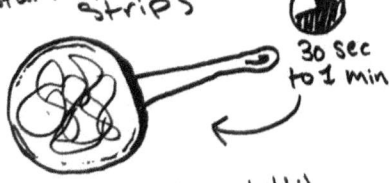

(It Looks Like Spaghetti)

Step 6

Fish out your film and put in a bowl of room tempature water

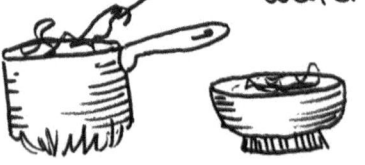

of the

Step 7

Find a Flat Somewhat Sharp object like an exacto blade, butter knife, or my fav, another peice of film.

trade

gently scrape along the cooked film to lift the emulsion into the water.

☆ if your really good you can get it off whole ☆

Step 8

take some film clear or even film that already has footage and dip it in the water. Find some emulsion and using your finger guide the film onto the leeder. this is hard so expect some failure.

Step 9

leave your film out to dry. once dry it will be very delacate so handle carefully and scan

⇒ASAP⇐

– Further Notes –

I am currently looking for a way to get the emulsion to stick better to the leeder. some ideas to try are...

→ gelatin layer on leeder?

→ Some kind of sealent maybe mod podge or spray?

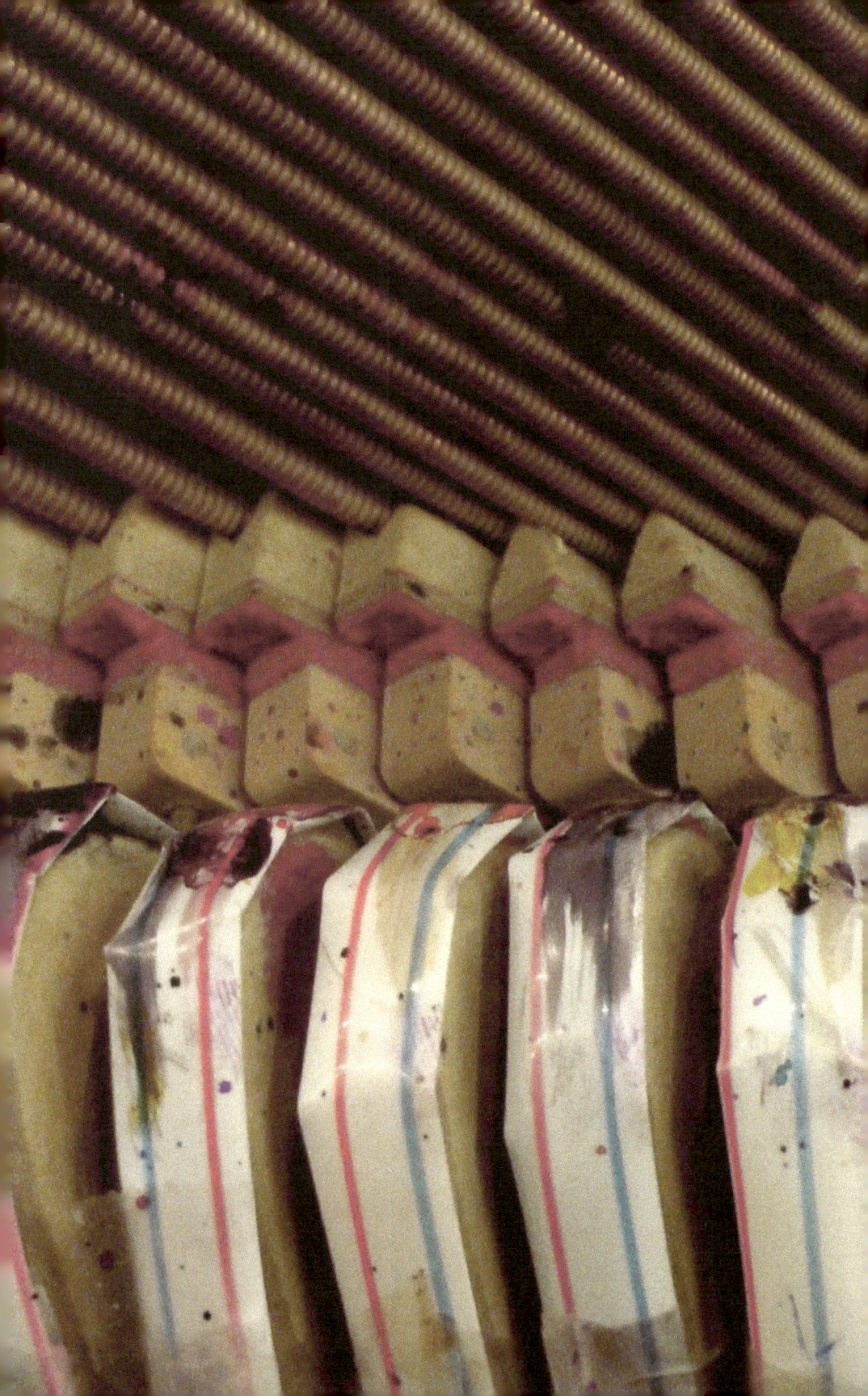

253' 11"

A "live" experimental film on 16mm and a farewell to my upright piano in the summer of 2016. The piano was modified to allow clear 16mm leader to run through the middle of the piano, between every hammer and set of strings, out the other side, through a projector, and onto a growing pile on the floor. A small "marker" made of a plastic straw, felt, and fast-drying alcohol ink was affixed to each hammer and then punctured, allowing it to mark the film with ink whenever its corresponding key was played. The color scheme of the white notes repeats within each octave (ABCDEFG -> ROYGBIV). The black notes all used black ink. There is 253' 11" of film between the first and last mark.

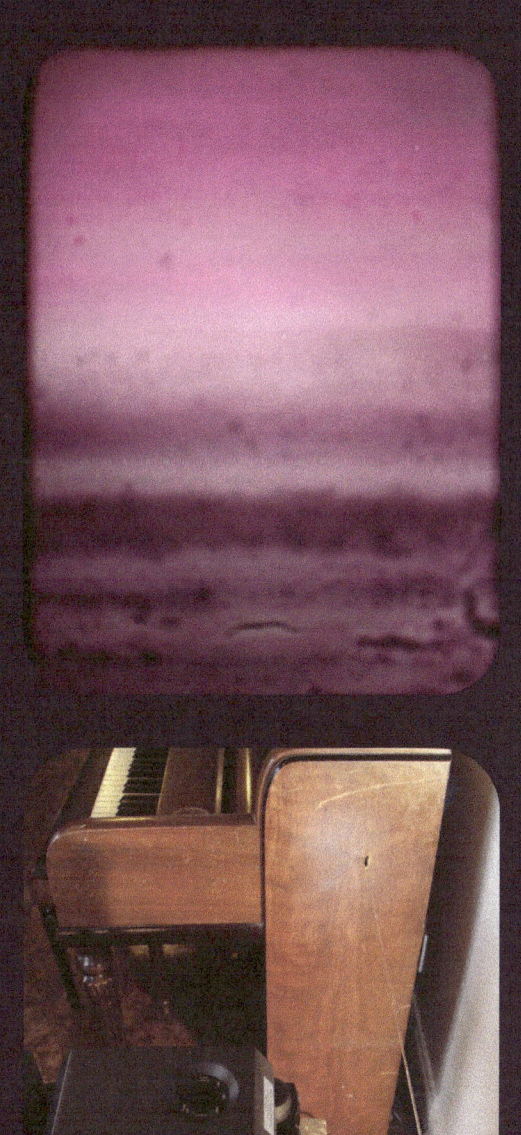

Auden Lincoln-Vogel

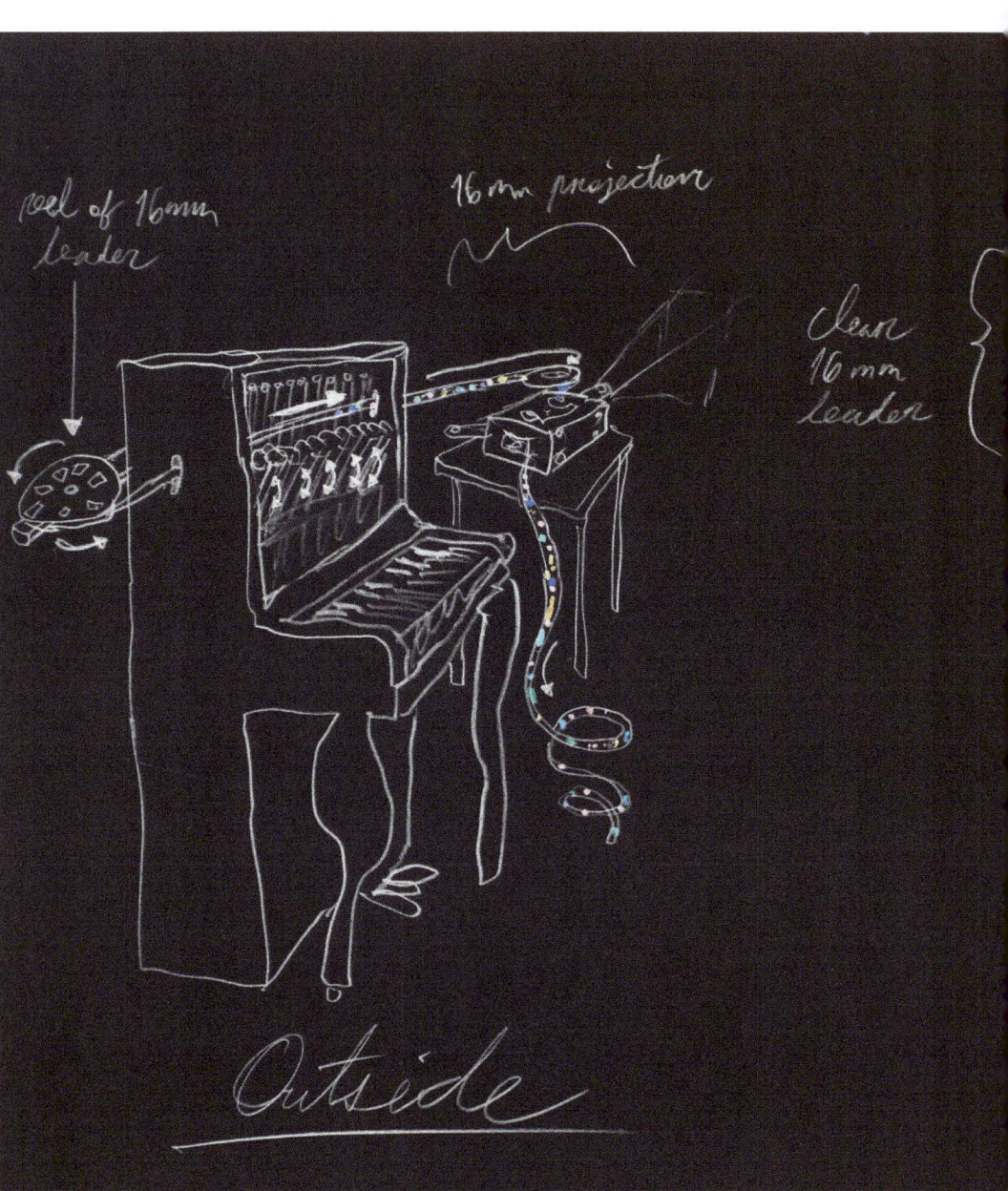

reel of 16mm
leader

16 mm projection

clean
16 mm
leader

Outside

100

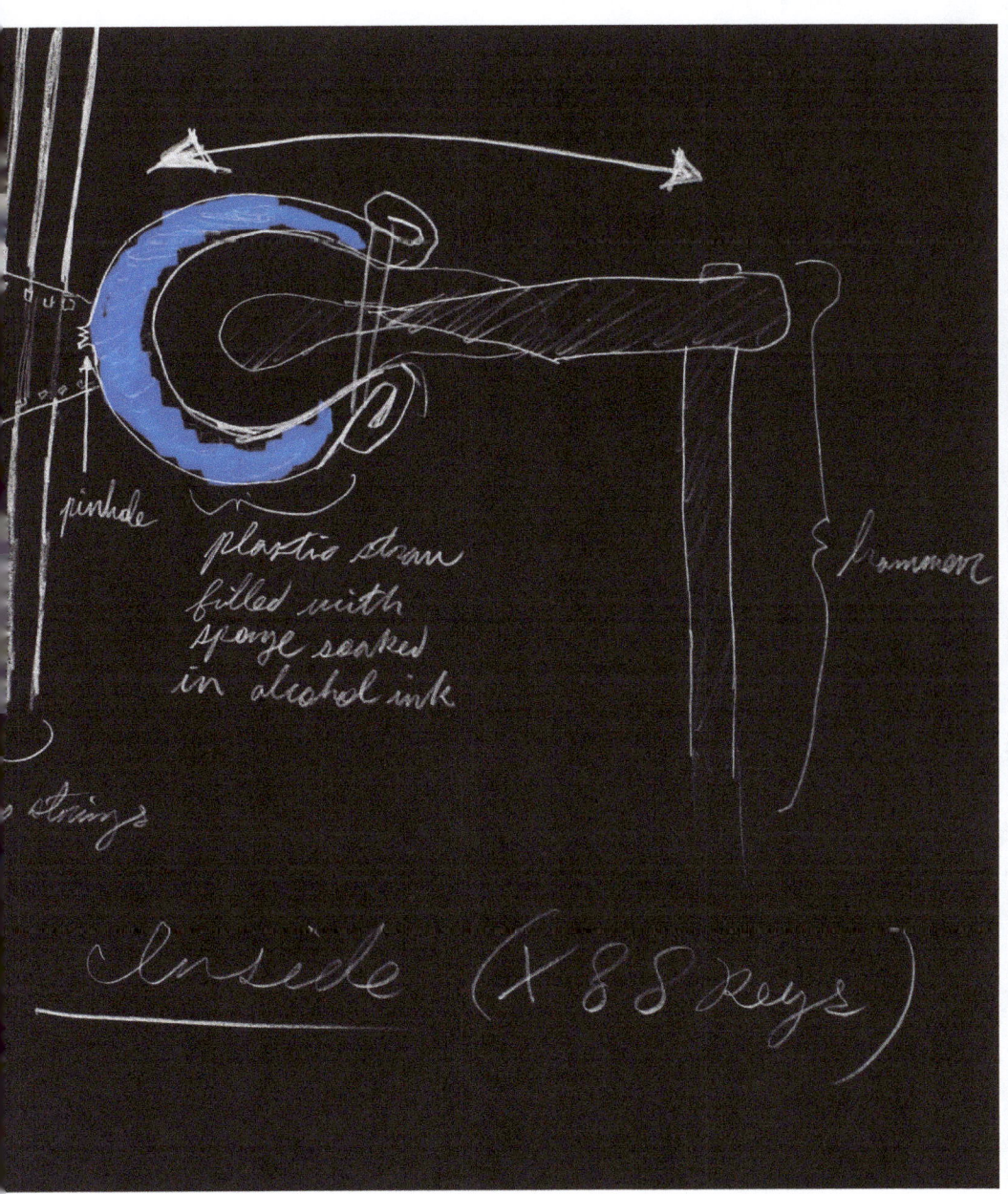

pinhole

plastic straw
filled with
sponge soaked
in alcohol ink

hammer

strings

Inside (X 88 keys)

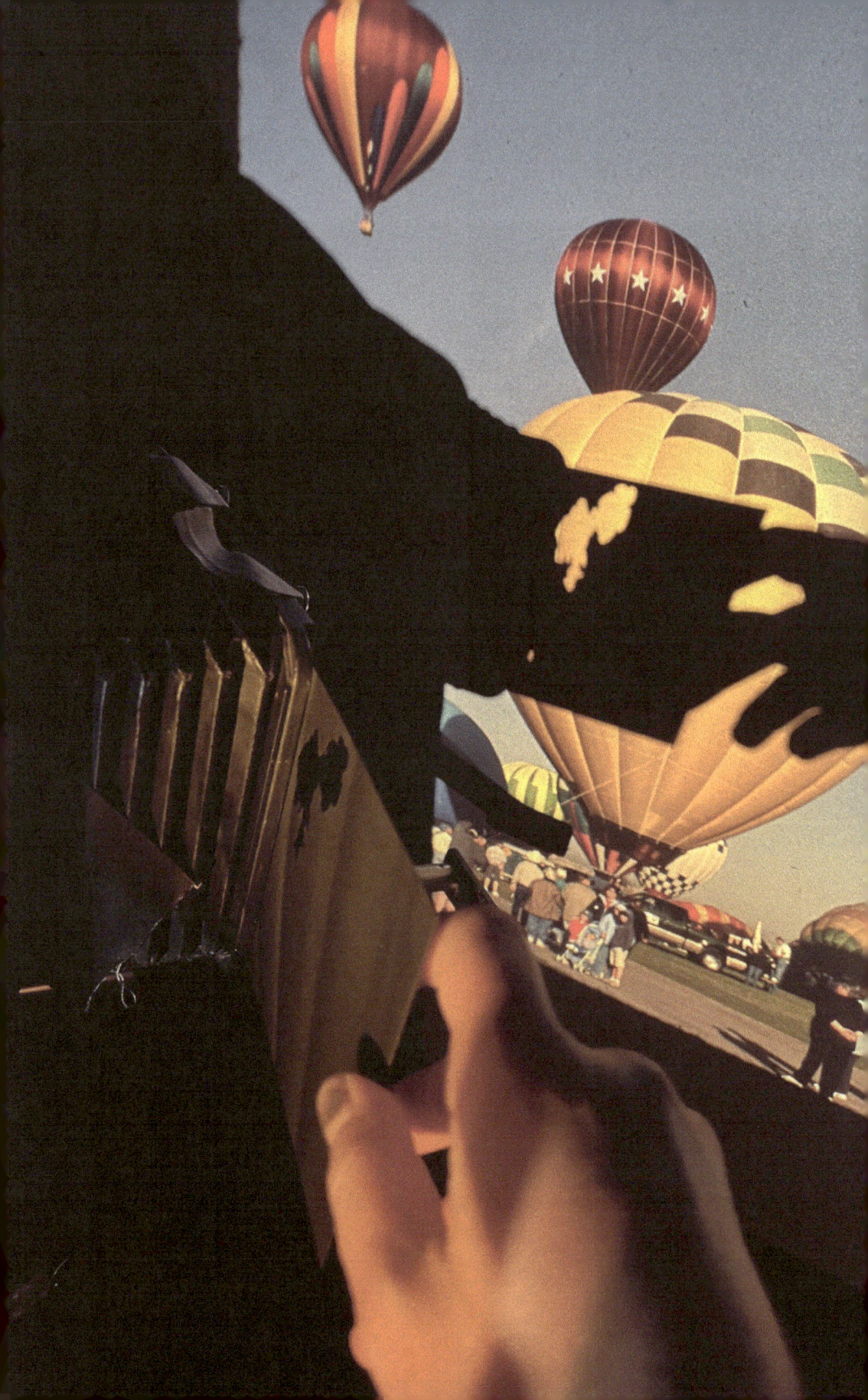

above / below, or How to Create a Rotoscope Animation with a Bolex Mattebox

Anna Hogg

Double Exposure and the View from Above/Below

I have been working with 16mm film for about 15 years, drawn to the material possibilities that analog processes offer—the depth, texture, and wonderfully unexpected artifacts that emerge through physical manipulation of the medium. For this project, I began exploring double exposures as a way to create images-within-the-image, partly inspired by Kurt Kren's 31/75: Asyl.

The Checkerboard Matte Process

I created a checkerboard-like matte for my first test, though where Kren's piece shows a landscape changing over time—some squares in winter, others in fall or spring—I was interested in the mini-frames-within-the-frame as discrete viewing windows. I took the Bolex to a hot air balloon festival in Albuquerque, filming hundreds of balloons taking off at once. Initially, I allowed a large balloon on the ground to fill parts of the frame in fragmented form, but once airborne, I framed the balloons moving in and out of the tiny boxes created by the matte.

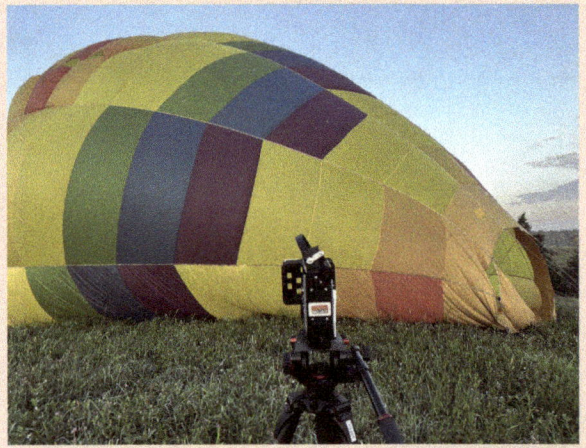

After rewinding the film, I changed out the matte for its negative and waited for inspiration to complete the second exposure. The technical constraint of the checkerboard pattern had created a formal structure, but I needed conceptual content to fill those remaining spaces.

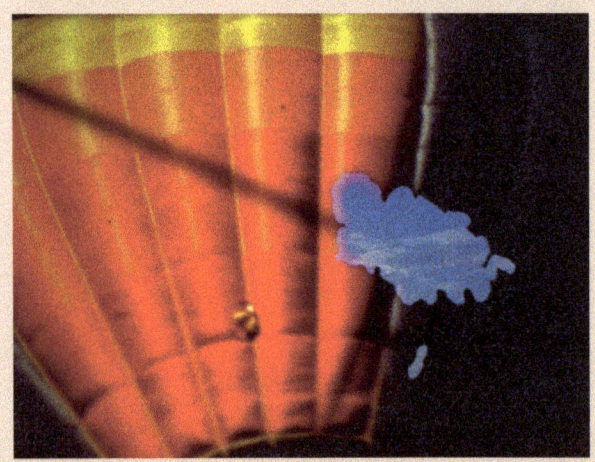

From Documentation to Speculation

At the time, my growing obsession with hot air balloons intersected with a news event: the Chinese surveillance balloon that crossed the United States in early 2023 before being shot down by the U.S. military off the coast of Myrtle Beach, South Carolina on February 4th, 2023. The balloon had been tracked by satellites, generating both military and public fascination with its movements.

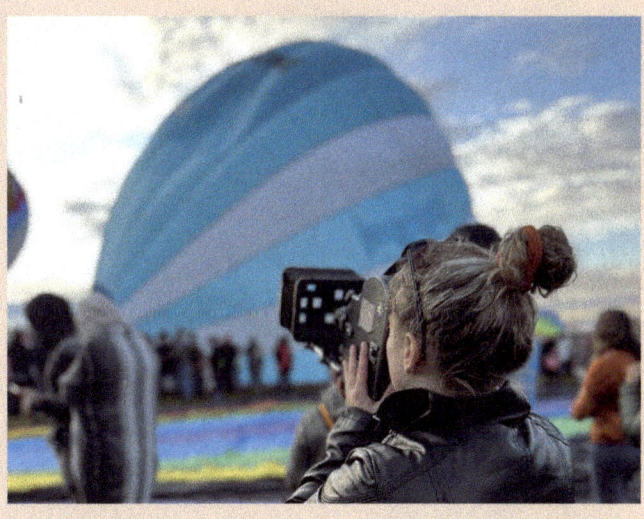

This suggested a compelling tension between perspectives: the view from below–public obsession and documentation of the surveillance balloon, mirroring my own fixation on hot air balloons–and the view from above–satellites tracking the balloon's movements from an even greater height. For the second exposure, I created a screen capture of my search through NASA's Landsat data, progressively "zooming in" to examine the site of the surveillance balloon's wreckage. At a certain magnification, no additional data was available, leaving only blocks of pixels that mirrored my checkerboard matte pattern.

This technical limitation became a narrative opportunity. The pixelated breakdown of the satellite imagery suggested the limits of surveillance itself–the point where documentation dissolves into abstraction. Here, the factual began to transform into the speculative.

The Speculative Turn

A parafictional narrative began to form. Instead of being recovered by the U.S. military, I imagined the balloon and its surveillance fragments sinking to the ocean floor, where they would merge with a deep-water coral reef known as Lophelia Pertusa. This coral exists in the aphotic zone, depths where no light penetrates. Rather than relying on photosynthetic processes like shallow-water corals, it feeds on plankton and organic matter–"marine snow"–that drifts down from above.

This coral reef actually exists: the Million Mounds, stretching off the southeastern United States on the Blake Plateau. But in my speculative version, the surveillance technology becomes integrated into this ecosystem, creating a cyborgian coral reef that embodies the intersection of natural and artificial systems.

Rotoscope as Special Effects

Rather than digital effects, I chose rotoscope animation to visualize this transformation. I traced the balloon's fall sequence, juxtaposing static 35mm slides of hot air balloons against clouds. The colorful balloons resembled flags of different nations, maritime signals, or—when flickering—warning sirens. Through this formal approach, I addressed the ubiquity of surveillance, questions of sovereignty and witness, and a more-than-human perspective.

The juxtaposition of different images-within-the-image allowed me to work in film similarly to how Dadaist photomontage functions—layering meaning through collision and contrast. I'm now working on another rotoscope sequence that traces a close-up tracking shot through the Million Mounds, using footage provided by Dr. Erik Cordes, who studies this coral's unusual resilience to climate change.

This project, titled "above / below," will eventually comprise three parts. The interviews I conducted with Dr. Cordes and Dr. Alexis Weinnig will feature heavily in part three, which explores the speculative cyborgian coral reef in greater depth.

LASER CUTTING MATTES FOR A BOLEX MATTEBOX

Equipment and Materials

Laser Cutter: Any machine capable of vector cutting through poster-board material. I worked with Universal Laser Systems cutters (50W-100W) at UVA Architecture School's FabLab (shout out to Melissa Goldman and Trevor Kemp!), but less powerful machines or smart cutters will work as long as they can cut precisely through poster-board.

Materials: Black poster-board (no foam core) or black card-stock (80lb minimum). Poster-board is recommended despite higher cost—card-stock is flimsy and difficult to handle.

Software: Adobe Illustrator (required for vector cutting)

Basic Matte Creation

Document Setup

Create a new Illustrator document: 32×18" (flatbed size), RGB color mode. Draw a rectangle 5.5×4.03" (sized for Bolex matte box) with 0.001" line weight in RGB cyan (#00ffff). This line weight and color are essential—the laser cutter is coded to recognize cyan vectors for cutting.

Creating the Positive Matte

1. Draw your desired shape using the pen tool or shape tools

2. Shapes can extend beyond the matte frame, but maintain a minimum 0.15" border connecting to the outer rectangle

3. Duplicate the entire matte to a new layer (this becomes your negative)

4. Select all shapes and use Shape Builder tool to connect them

5. Delete any extraneous shapes outside the outer rectangle

6. Delete all paths except the single complex shape that forms your matte

7. Ensure one continuous path connects all elements

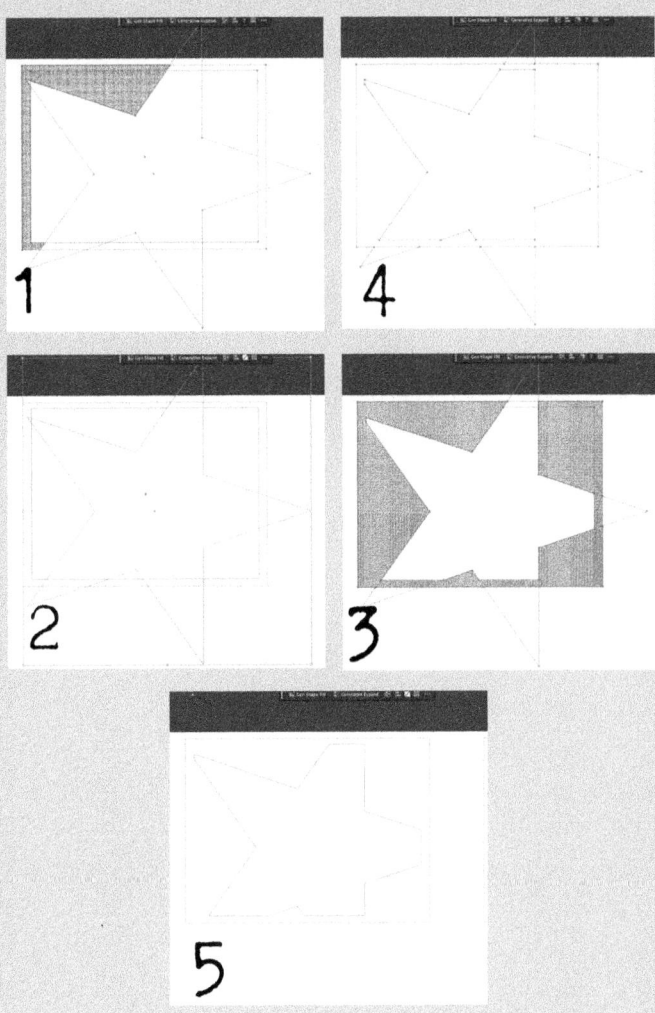

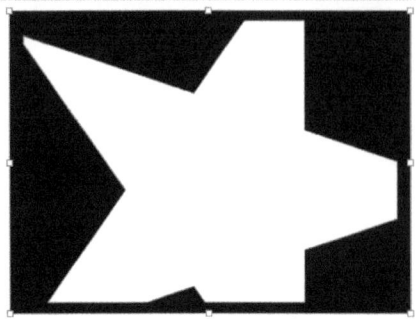 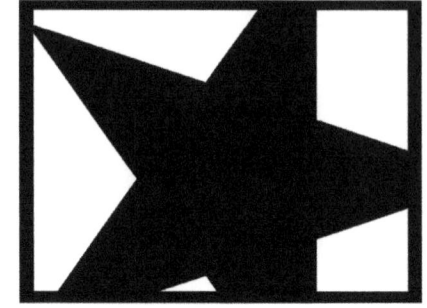

Creating the Negative Matte

1. Work with your duplicated layer
2. For circles or holes in the center, create connecting points to the outer rectangle
3. Delete all paths except the single complex shape that forms your matte
4. Ensure one continuous path connects all elements

Laser Cutting Process

Material Preparation

Cut poster-board to 18×32" if working with larger sheets. Arrange multiple mattes side by side with minimal spacing–approximately 20 mattes fit per sheet.

Machine Settings

Use factory recommendations for Power, Speed, and PPI for poster-board. Focus the laser to your material using the bed adjustment tool. Poster-board is among the thinnest materials for laser cutting.

Troubleshooting

→ If cuts don't go through completely: decrease speed slightly or increase power slightly
→ Avoid over-adjustment–too slow or too much power will burn the material
→ Keep X-acto blade and self-healing mat ready for minor touch-ups

Rotoscoping Process

Sequence Selection

Choose sequences with high contrast that will remain recognizable as cutout shapes. Limit to 200 frames maximum due to time intensity. Examples that work well:

→ White balloons against blue sky
→ White coral against dark sea background

Illustrator Setup for Animation

1.Layer Organization:

→ Middle layer: rectangular matte frame
→ Bottom layer: image sequence (import all frames at once)
→ Top layers: Individual layers for each traced frame (001, 002, etc.)

2. Image Import:

→ Drag entire image sequence into Illustrator simultaneously into the Image Sequence layer on the bottom

→ Resize all images to fit within rectangular frame for your matte

→ Turn off all images except the first frame (the linked file on the bottom)

→ This prevents registration issues

Tracing Process

1. Manual Tracing: Use pen tool rather than Image Trace to maintain vector control

2. Line Weight: Work at cutting thickness (0.001") to preserve image nuances

3. No Fill: Use outline only during tracing

4. Frame-by-Frame:

→ Create new layer for each frame
→ Copy and paste-in-place from previous frame (Shift + Command + V)
→ Turn on next image in sequence
→ Adjust pen tool path accordingly

Creating Positive Rotoscope Mattes

1. Save original file, then work in duplicate

2. Delete image sequence layer
3. Copy and paste-in-place the rectangular frame to each traced layer

4. Add border edges where shapes extend beyond matte confines

5. Use Shape Builder tool to connect shapes to outer matte edge

6. Test by filling shapes with black to verify positive/negative areas

Creating Negative Rotoscope Mattes

1. Repeat process for negative version

2. Add connecting points for any "floating" shapes

3. Ensure single continuous path connects all elements within the matte

4. Each frame should result in one unified vector path

Technical Notes

→ Different laser cutters may use different color codes–test or consult lab recommendations

→ Registration is critical for rotoscope work–import all images simultaneously to avoid positioning errors

→ Label your mattes with the frame number (white pencil) on the side that faces away from the lens

→ The process is time-intensive but allows for precise, custom animated mattes impossible to achieve through other means

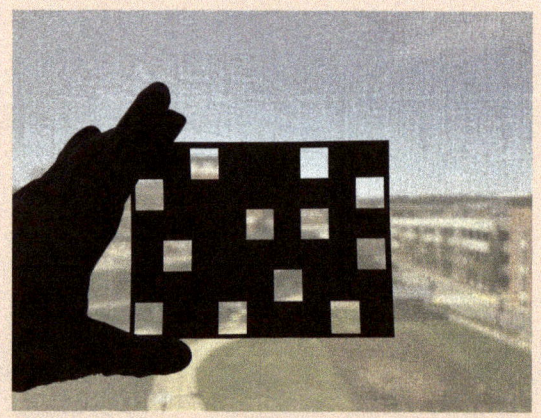

Filming Process

Choosing your subjects

Think about what images will be juxtaposed through this process. Some questions to consider include:

→ How do the two parts of the image connect to each other conceptually?

→ How are the two images different in terms of color, texture, micro/macro, etc.?

→ How recognizable will the subject be in fragmented form?

Aligning the Matte Box

1. Extend the bellows of the matte box to the desired distance

2. Tape in place - it is imperative that the matte box not move forward or back

3. Insert matte into track (There are two tracks, so use the same one each time)

4. Make sure the matte is completely inserted so as to ensure correct registration

5. Repeat for the number of frames

Filming

1. Use the frame counter on the Bolex to track your frame number

2. Keep a detailed log in a notebook

3. Create single frames for each positive (or negative matte)

4. Rewind the Bolex using rewind tool (make sure to cover lens and viewfinder)

5. Repeat the process for the negative matte, following your log for the first part of the filming process

Technical Notes

Instead of completing the rotoscope process in camera, you can composite the positive and negative mattes digitally. This allows you to be less precise when filming and to fix any potential mistakes.

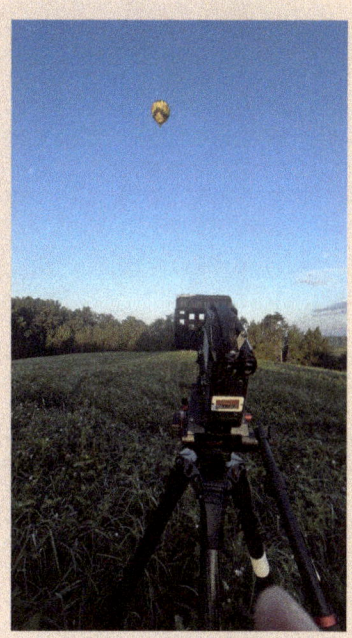

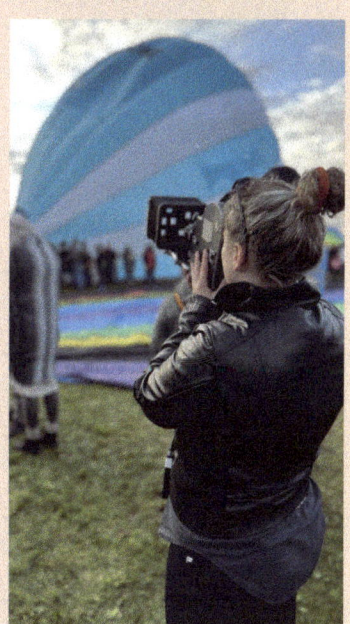

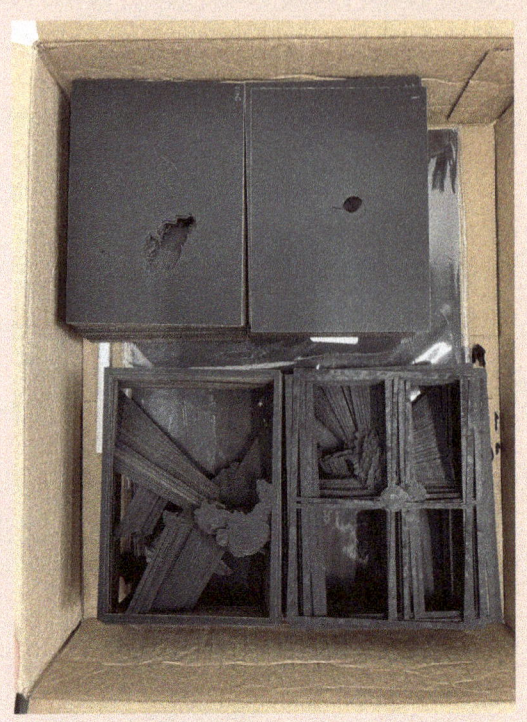

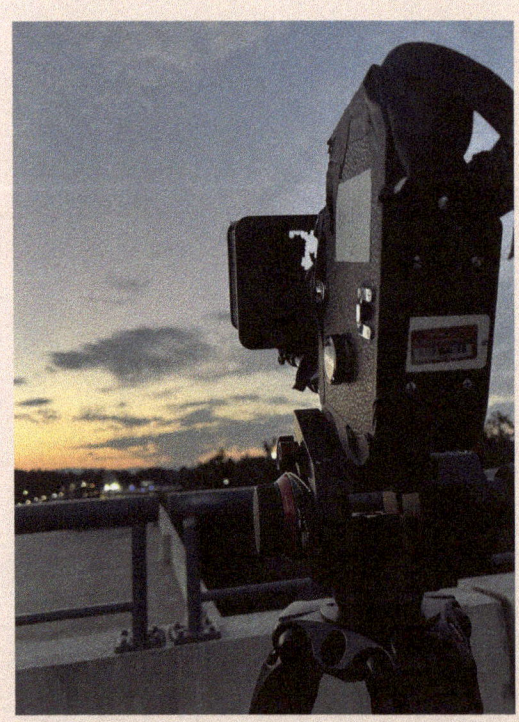

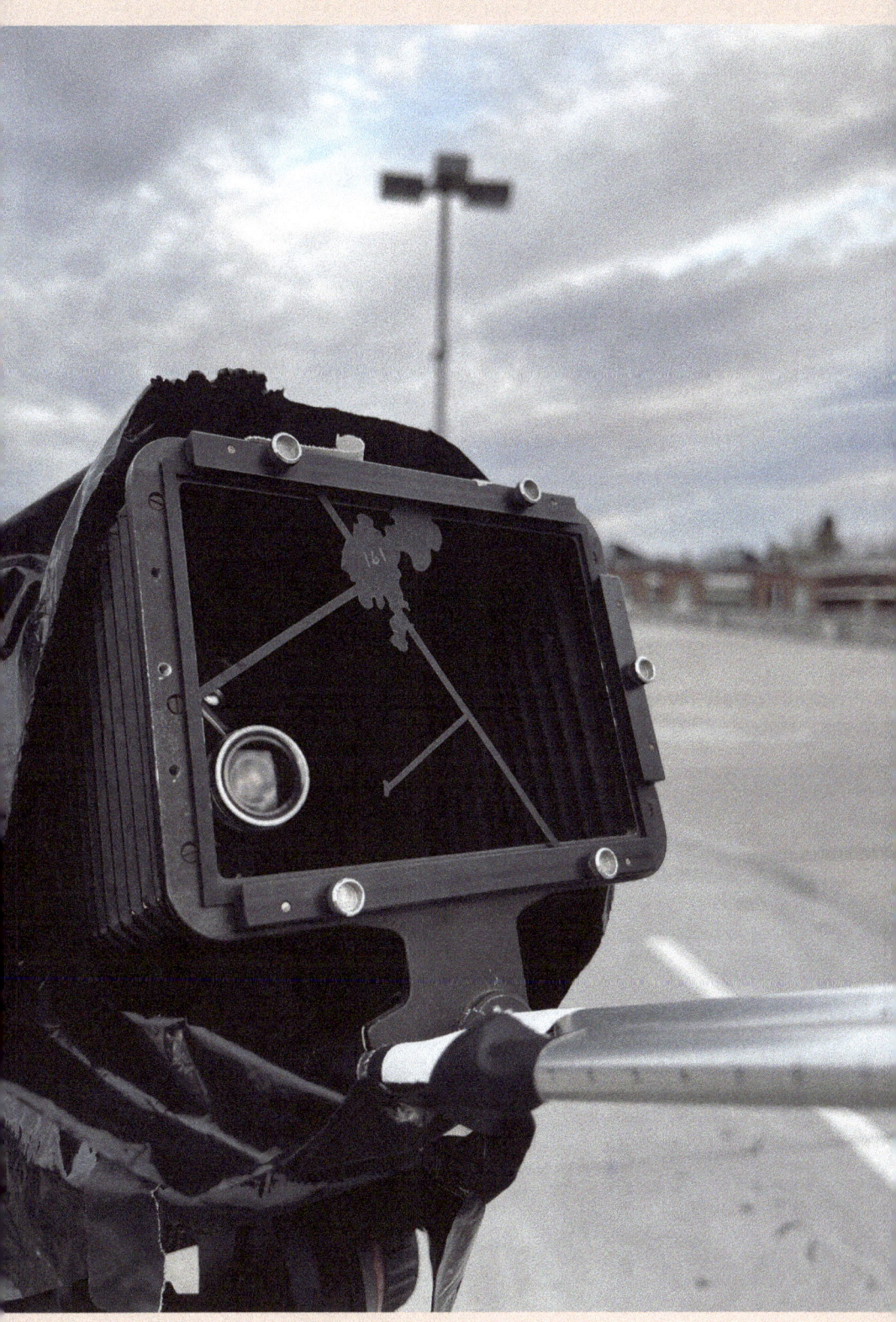

How To Make Animation Into a Sewing Circle

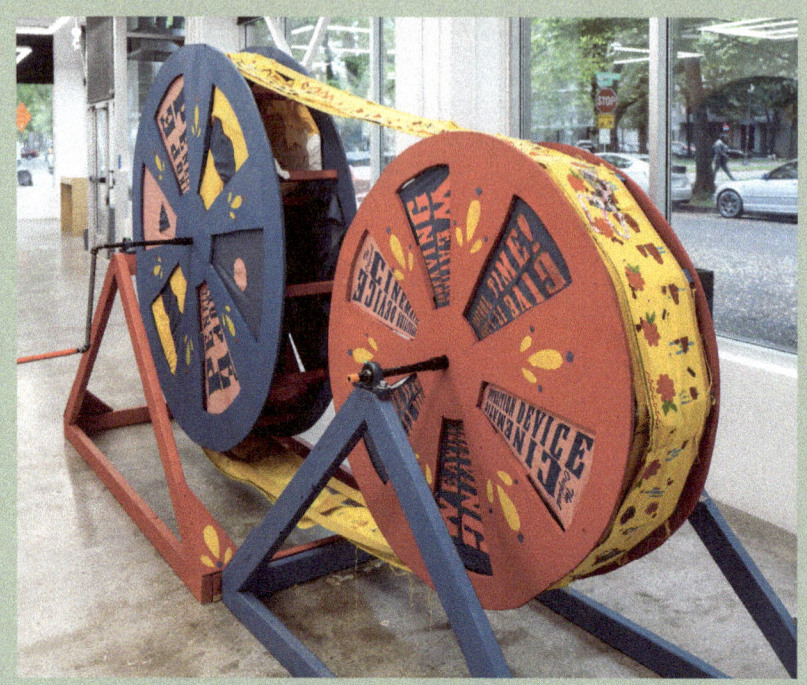

Charlie C Wilcox

This is a recipe for my own form of fusion film-cuisine that takes ingredients from modes of animation and textile handcraft practices and melds them into a hybrid form I've named the Fabric Film Strip. As someone who had developed concurrent interests in experimental animation and traditional needlecraft, I wondered what it would look like to transfer some of the community-minded lineages of textile arts to the sphere of animation. Early in my animation journey, as I weighed the options available to me as an "animator," it seemed that the main two options were to join the industry and work for a studio, or to develop my practice as a studio artist-animator, and there wasn't a lot of space outside of these options to incorporate animation into one's life as a craft, or hobby, or something not so all-consuming as a career either independently or for a studio. I don't want to be overly binary, as there is, of course, a lineage of animation that separates itself from those two options, but opportunities to engage with communal, radically-minded animation are somewhat sparse. I couldn't help but feel that the field of animation lacked some of the traits and affordances that allow for many forms of craft and artmaking, like embroidery, to emerge and proliferate as authentic, participatory forms of social artmaking. By mixing fabric arts into an animation process, I hope to show how animation can be made more accessible to a wider range of folks as participants, and not just viewers.

The concept of the Fabric Film Strip came to life from that idea as an intermediary between direct animation and sewing circles. The Fabric Film Strip is a long loop of fabric that could be acted upon by multiple people at once, creating a shared, animated piece of visual storytelling not predetermined but emerging from the collaborating hands of the participants. Many of the appealing qualities of direct animation are easy to identify; it is a method that is relatively accessible and affordable, has a fairly low skill barrier to entry, and can be viewed in process or final form immediately (provided you have a projector handy). Perhaps the only significant challenge that direct animation provides, for my purposes, comes from the size and scale of celluloid itself. It can be challenging to get a group of people huddled around one piece of filmstock and working together. Sure, there are ways around this, by suturing together individuals' pieces of hand-altered film, or building workflows and specific jobs around different steps of the direct animation process, but to get a group of people together and building one piece of animation on a shared canvas, the most obvious step would be to jump to a larger, scalable material.

Step 1: Prepare the Fabric

I usually use 3.5-4 yards of fabric per film strip. Linen is my preferred variety, as the crosshatching of the threads in linen shows up nicely once animated, almost replicating the scratches and visual grit of celluloid. Simple cotton yardage works well too. In the most basic version of a Fabric Film Strip, you could simply cut the fabric in equal strips—I aim for 11-12" wide per cut— and sew these individual strips together into a loop, and call it good. (I won't necessarily be so granular as to walk through how to sew fabric together or other such details, and hopefully you'll forgive me for these omissions. I will note that I favor hand-stitching in nearly all situations, so I'll use embroidery floss to attach these strips together in a loop, but by all means, use a sewing machine if you have one handy).

I've found, however, that constructing some form of base layer of animation on the Fabric Film Strip helps participants more effectively visualize the piece of fabric in front of them as a piece of filmic material. Especially for those that haven't had much experience animating before, visualizing individual frames becomes easier when they can see how far a shape 'moves' from frame to frame, and at the very least, frame markers allow one to visually triangulate the space of the fabric animation frame. This base layer can be as simple or ornate as you'd like—in the first handful of workshops I led, I screenprinted a full-fledged 'background' for the animation, which took the form of ovoid shapes that moved in and out of the frame in a looping pattern. The groups of shapes move on the X and Y axis specifically for the sake of providing participants with that metric of movement as it will happen. This was a very time-intensive process of preparation, and as such I wouldn't necessarily recommend doing something quite this ornate unless you already have a bit of experience in screenprinting and the requisite facilities available to you.

A much simpler and more forgiving approach would be to stencil frames onto the fabric using Duralar and screenprinting ink. This method of blockprinting was taught to me as a cost-effective option alternative to screenprinting that can be done basically anywhere; you can spread out your fabric and get a little messy. Duralar is a type of sturdy, frosted transparency film that you can pick up at many art stores, upon which frame guides can be traced and cut out, which you can then ink onto the fabric repeatedly. This mainly requires a bit of measuring—if your fabric strip is ~12" across, and you want the frames to have a standard widescreen aspect ratio of 16:9, giving yourself a little wiggle room on the fringes of the strip would allow for frames of about ~11.5" wide and ~6.5" tall (one could be more exact on measurements, I guess, but this type of handmade filmmaking need not necessarily be an exact science.) What I've done, with those measurements, is cut out plus sign-shaped marks at each corner, and when I print them on the fabric, just overlay the top marks from the frame below to the bottom marks of the subsequent frame. In order to print using the

stencil, you can use a simple foam brush, just be careful not to pull up the stencil as you are brushing and deposit screenprinting ink on the underside of the stencil, globbing up your fabric.

If that sounds daunting, you could do something as simple as drawing frame lines with a fabric pen or marker, measuring out the height of your frame with a ruler. It's all your prerogative as a facilitator. For example, in the Fabric Film Strip workshop I led with City Repair's Village Building Convergence, a place-making festival here in Portland, I block-printed an abstract, looping outline of a sidewalk using just three different stencils and employing the above method, creating the suggestion of walking down a city street. This fed into a prompt for the workshop for participants to envision what they want to see on their streets and add it to the animation. When I led a workshop with a printmaking class at Willamette University, on the other hand, the students had a stock of linocut designs they had already made, so I didn't need to prepare the films strip with anything more than simple hash marks, as the students were able to quickly fill up the frames with easily repeated stamps.

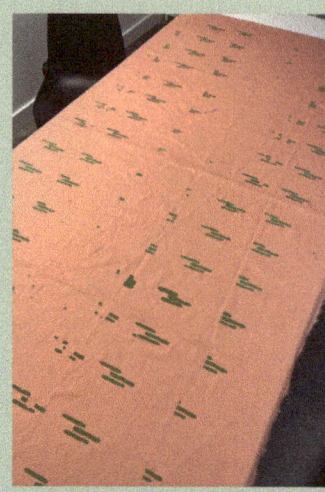

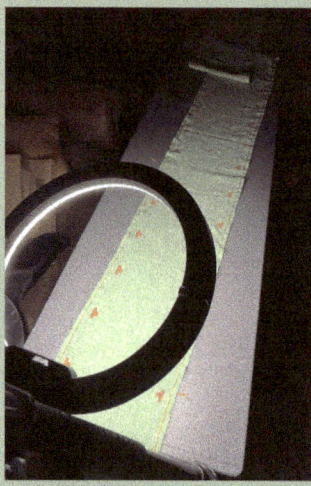

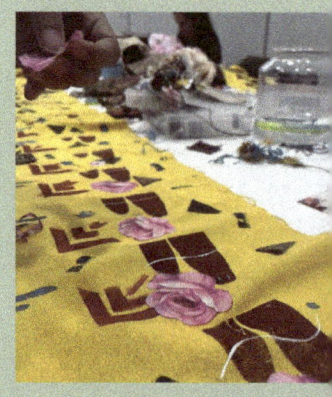

Step 2: Prepare the Animation

After I put the film strip together in a physical sense, I'll usually animate the 'blank' strip before anything is added to it. This is more important if you've added anything to the body of the frames as background or setting for the animation, but can serve a few purposes even if the only thing you are animating are frame markers and fabric. Some Fabric Film Strip workshops that I've led have had multiple sessions, which I prefer for multiple reasons. First and foremost, it allows me as the facilitator/animator to photograph the Fabric Film Strip between sessions, capturing an iterative development of the animation over time, which then feeds back into the subsequent workshops, as participants can see the loop of animation in progress, giving them more ideas as to how and what to add to the piece. Having multiple sessions also allows for a greater range of participation, allowing people to drop in as much or little as they would like, providing a scalable commitment level.

When you are working with 3.5-4 yards of fabric and the proportions discussed above, the resulting Fabric Film Strip usually has around 80-90 individual frames per loop, roughly seven seconds of screen time if you are animating on twos (two images captured per frame, a fairly standard stop-motion animation practice). This isn't particularly long, so multiple iterative loops helps to beef up the final animation. It is instructive for participants, however, to see the relationship between the amount of input (30-40 feet of fabric) to output (seven seconds of runtime) and see just how much labor and material goes into any animation or handmade filmmaking process.

Step 3: Prepare the Tools

The other aspect of preparing for a Fabric Film Strip workshop is gathering materials for participants to use to alter and manipulate the film strip. This is vastly customizable, and I'm sure there are many potential tools that I haven't even thought of using. A crucial affordance of fabric, especially in comparison to celluloid, is the sheer number of extant practices available to draw upon from the world of textile craft, as well as the relative workability of fabric as a material. For how great traditional direct animation is, it can still be reliant on being able to get the celluloid through the projector, and the celluloid can only take so much creative damage before it risks falling apart.

As an embroiderist, that practice tends to be my home base for fabric animation, so I am able to supply a large collection of flosses, hoops, and needles. Ordering yourself a box of children's scissors would serve you well here. I'm generally on the lookout for caches of fabric samples in the secondhand market, or from the wonderful craft recycle store Scrap here in Portland, as these often quirky designs make great material to cut into shapes and quilt onto the fabric. Cutting out a handful of vaguely similar shapes and sewing them on subsequent frames is a bit more expeditious than embroidering the same design at the same scale, too, which comes into play if you only have a limited amount of time during the workshop. Depending on the context, I'll also supply screenprinting inks and paintbrushes, although I've avoided this in settings that we can't get quite as messy.

Step 4: Set Up the Space

You'll have to work with the space available when it comes to this step, but the increased scale of the Fabric Film Strip does require a decently sized space for people to be able to work on. If you have at least a few tables you can put together, that should do the trick. I generally like to arrange the film strip to loop around the edge of the table, and spread the supplies listed above in the middle of the circle. This ensures that participants are choreographed to sit in that circle, facing each other, nurturing engagement with each other rather than retreating into their own worlds.

The other step is getting my camera rig and computer set up so that animation examples can be shown, either of the blank Film Strip or prior work. Setting this up also allows you to transition from crafting to an animation demo relatively quickly. If there's a projector in your space, make use of it.

Snacks are, if permitted in your space, never a bad idea.

Step 5: Conduct the Workshop

While this is, of course, the most important step of the Fabric Film Strip process, it's also the step for which I have the least proscriptive guidance. For as many facilitators there are in the world, there are just as many facilitation styles, and you'll have to develop an approach that you find comfortable and

works for the project you have in mind.

Step 6: Make The Animation

Depending on the specific focus of the workshop or direct interest of the participants, I'll usually end a Fabric Film Strip workshop by demoing how to use Dragonframe and photograph the strip for animation purposes, but not necessarily perform the entire process for an audience, so I'll allot 15-30 minutes to do that at the end of the session. Folks that participate in these workshops have been, in my experience, interested in the act of stop-motion animation, and so showing them an example of how to interface between the software, the camera, and the film strip goes a long way, but there's not a need to have them sit and watch me animate the entire thing.

Step 7: Post-Production

It is crucial to my artistic beliefs that everyone who contributes to a Fabric Film Strip is credited equally as a creative collaborator on the project, and I make sure to include those credits in the final version of the animation. That's the one finishing touch that I require of the Fabric Film Strip projects that I lead. From there, where the Fabric Film Strip 'lives'

has been variable. I've led workshops where the physical Film Strip and the animation are shown in a gallery immediately afterwards, and other workshops where the animation is shared digitally via an organization's social media. At the very least, the animation should get sent out to the participants. To show these Film Strips in a gallery setting, I built the Peneletrope Cinematic Opposition Device, a conceptual film projector by way of kinetic sculpture, but that's a whole other story. I envision a particularly intriguing way to show the Film Strips would be to invert them and line the circumference of a room with the Film Strip, so you can be "inside" the strip and walk around the individual frames. In the end, I hope that the continued existence of the Fabric Film Strip creates a meaningful, instigating interruption in the way we receive and interact with animation and filmmaking as a form, breaking us out of established forms to a new practice that inspires new creativities and new collaborations across media. Even as the Film Strips strive for those lofty goals, it's just as great to be able to sit together with a new group of people and stitch for the afternoon. I hope you'll join me sometime, or give it a try on your own.

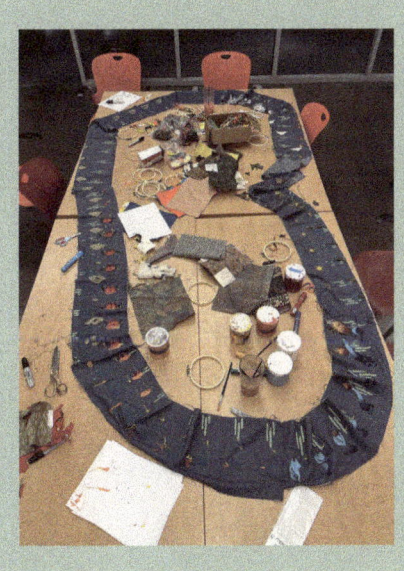

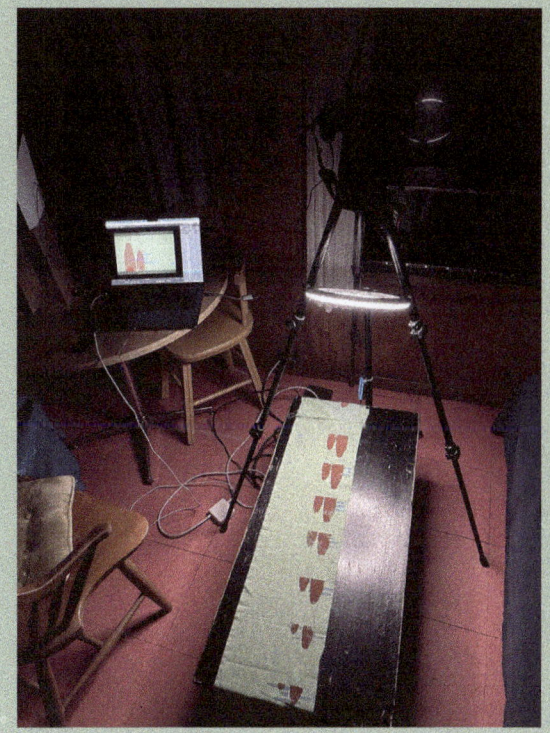

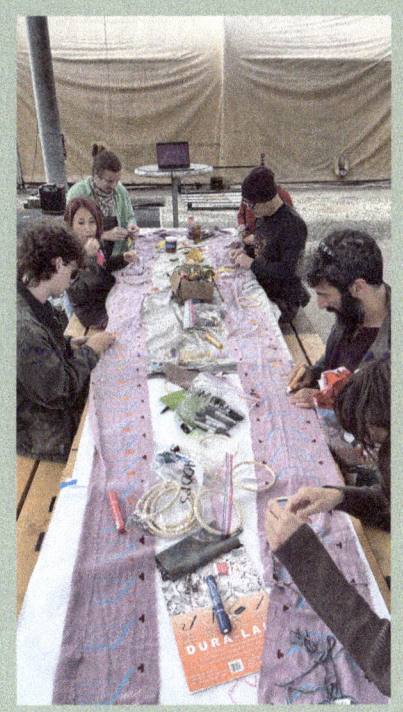

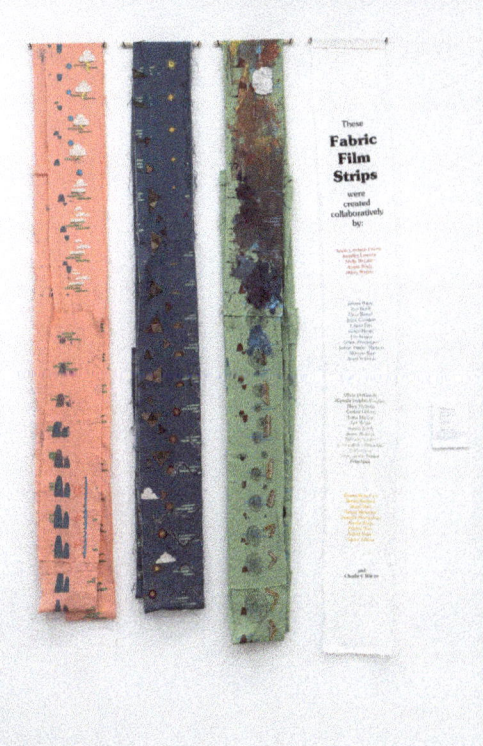

These
Fabric
Film
Strips
were
created
collaboratively
by:

www.ingramcontent.com/pod-product-compliance
Lightning Source LLC
Chambersburg PA
CBHW040111180526
45172CB00010B/1303